BEL-TIB NEW BOOKS
720.9794 Heimann 2001
Heimann, Jim, 1948-
California crazy and
beyond : roadside
vernacular architecture
31111021545502   7/01

CALIFORNIA CRAZY
AND BEYOND

ROADSIDE VERNACULAR ARCH

JIM HEIMANN

D1119497

Copyright © 2001 by Jim Heimann.
All rights reserved. No part of this book
may be reproduced in any form without
written permission from the publisher.

Library of Congress
Cataloging-in-Publication Data:

Heimann, Jim, 1948 —
    California crazy and beyond : road-
side vernacular architecture / by Jim
Heimann; introduction by David
Gebhard.
    p. cm.

ISBN 0-8118-3018-7
1. Architecture—California.
2. Architecture, Modern—20th
    century—California.
3. Vernacular architecture—California.
4. Roadside architecture—California.
    I. Title.

NA730.C2 H39 2001
720'.9794—dc 21 00-057085
Printed in Hong Kong.

Distributed in Canada by
Raincoast Books
9050 Shaughnessy Street
Vancouver, BC V6P 6E5

Chronicle Books LLC
85 Second Street
San Francisco, California
94105
www.chroniclebooks.com

10 9 8 7 6 5 4 3 2 1

Book Design by Jim Heimann
Digital Composition by Cindy Vance

Frontispiece: A rare view of a programmatic building under construction, the fourth Chili Bowl, 5061
Whittier Boulevard, ca 1932. *Above:*
Purity of form meets the realities of
the marketplace. The Pup,
12728 Washington Boulevard, ca
1940. Photograph by Ansel Adams.

TABLE OF
CONTENTS

FOREWORD   4

INTRODUCTION BY DAVID GEBHARD   6

CHAPTER 1   19

CALIFORNIA CRAZY

CHAPTER 2   113

OUT-OF-STATE ODDITIES

CHAPTER 3   161

SIGNS, CARS, AND GIANTS

CHAPTER 4   169

CURRENT CONDITION

LEGACY   175

INDEX   176

GEBHARD'S NOTES   178

PHOTO CREDITS   178

BIBLIOGRAPHY   179

ACKNOWLEDGMENTS   180

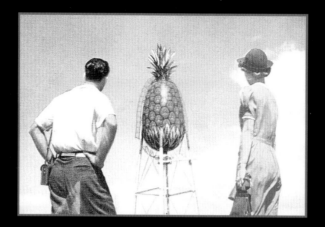

It was over twenty years ago that the first edition of *California Crazy* was published. The modest little book that sought to shed light on an obscure footnote to architectural history became over time the catalyst for renewed interest in roadside architecture, a textbook for architectural courses, and a passion for a subculture of oddball building aficionados. In the intervening years public recognition of these types of buildings not only increased, but resulted in a limited revival of programmatic architecture. Thanks to this revival hundreds of new images have surfaced, many of which reveal yet another layer of this architectural style.

This new edition of *California Crazy* maintains the pursuit for vernacular roadside architecture, aided of course by countless collectors and chroniclers of California Crazy images. As these pictures accumulated over the years, it became obvious that the majority of these buildings are still in California. Yet, they can be found all over the United States as well. The inclusion of oversized advertising signs and statues as an adjunct to the architectural examples seemed appropriate as an extension of the California Crazy concept. The same goes for automobiles that emulate fanciful objects. Though not architectural in nature, they follow the same obvious response to the zaniness that allows for roadside architectural extremes yet fall outside the boundaries of *California Crazy and Beyond.*

Domestic architecture, while not considered in the first edition, is marginally included here to

Above. **Dole pineapple water tower, Honolulu, Hawaii, 1927.**

serve as point of reference in showing how both commercial and private architecture influenced each other.

Finding an appropriate name for the many shaped and quizzical buildings found in *California Crazy and Beyond* has been a tough task. David Gebhard, in his introduction to the first edition of *California Crazy*, came up with the term *Programatic* (his spelling) to describe this type of architecture. While this name has given the style credence in an architectural context, it has failed to catch on or be clearly understood by the average Joe. The vernacular nature of the buildings seems to lose something in high art language. Categorizing them as bizarre, oddball, Pop, architectural aberrations, mimetic, unusual, or even humorous makes sense, but the all-encompassing word for this style remains elusive. Suggestions are welcome.

The discovery of so many more images of unusual buildings further substantiated the idea that Southern California was indeed the locus of this architectural subcategory. The original edition of this book alluded to the fact that the media had focused on a dozen or so buildings and distorted the actual number that existed. In fact, dozens more of these structures were built. Los Angeles' physical being has also contributed to the confusion. The geographic range of over 450 square miles often diluted a concentrated effect, and although these types of buildings did not literally line the streets, their numbers could not be duplicated in any comparable metropolitan area. When you take into consideration the more subtle examples of period-revival architecture, advertising sculptures, miniature golf courses, and houses in their various mutations and styles, one realizes that Los Angeles is a rather unusual place in comparison to the rest of the world.

Tracking down additional information about structures, some of which had disappeared eighty years ago, was a tough task. Several of the more difficult locations came to light after the first edition of *California Crazy* was published. Many buildings were located by long searches through newspaper microfilm in which ads or real estate announcements gave clues to the locations. I often checked an address and business name magnified from a photo against vintage telephone books and yellow pages. For instance, I located the Toonerville Trolley (1929) from an old matchbook cover. Menus,

captions from photo albums, and miscellaneous ephemera all provided clues or locations. I located the Hollywood Flower Pot (ca 1930) eventually when a reader insisted that he knew the building was on Vine Street just north of Santa Monica Boulevard because he had lived in it. His family, having moved to Hollywood during the Depression, found the Hollywood Flower Pot converted to a one-room residence and promptly moved in!

Interviews with the few remaining building owners reflected something in the human spirit—a desire to express oneself—that resulted in something as concrete as the buildings themselves. That spirit extended beyond Southern California, where I found innumerable examples of similar buildings, structures, and signs that prompted me to expand the "Out-of-State Oddities" chapter. Enlarging the scope of the book to include additional categories was like opening a can of worms. Confirming that buildings, signs, and giants existed in a specific location is a near impossible task. The rate at which these artifacts are moved, destroyed, or remodeled combined with the geographic range they cover precludes an accurate confirmation of their existence. But there is help out there: The Internet provides a lot of concrete information. Invaluable is the roadsideamerica.com site, which manages to keep track of all categories of the *California Crazy* stuff we love. Check it out if you're looking for confirmation of an existing artifact or an update about a favorite one.

I am convinced that the release of this volume will lead to the discovery of many more of these buildings, not only in California, but in the rest of the forty-nine states as well, thereby giving an even clearer picture of the world of oddball architecture. It is impossible to know just how many of these buildings were built, and the task of editing the images is always difficult. In these pages, I tried to represent the best of what existed and what remains today. With several thousand images to choose from, the edit eliminated a good chunk of what I dug up. Undoubtedly a favorite of yours is missing and for that I apologize. But that leaves room for another edition somewhere down the line as, hopefully, even more of these examples are discovered. Happy hunting.

Jim Heimann

Introduction by David Gebhard

David Gebhard, who died in 1996, was a pivotal player in the understanding and replacement of programmatic architecture into its rightful place in architectural history. In his essay in the first edition of California Crazy, *Gebhard coined the descriptive word Programatic (Gebhard used this spelling in his essay, but the current usage is "programmatic") to define this type of unconventional architecture and provided a template for the study of the subject, which was once considered unnecessary and ephemeral by many. It is included in this current edition because of its timelessness and as a tribute to a historian who clearly defined many architectural subjects others were unwilling to consider.*

"If, when you went shopping, you found you could buy cakes in a windmill, ices in a gigantic cream-can, flowers in a huge flowerpot, you might begin to wonder whether you had not stepped through a looking glass or taken a toss down a rabbit burrow and could expect Mad Hatter or White Queen to appear round the next corner. But there would be nothing unreal about it if you were in Hollywood, South California, for shops of that kind are to be seen in all the shopping districts there."[1] This reaction in the late 1930s by a Briton to Southern California is just one of the times the Southland has been viewed as the land of exotica. From the 1870s on, that which has seemed startling and unique in Southern California has been cultivated by both natives and visitors so that myth has slowly become fact.

In the late nineteenth century the exotica of Southern California almost always cited were its tropical and semi-tropical vegetation which had been introduced to the land, and what seemed to be a looser, more carefree, mode of daily life. By the mid-1880s the exuberance (or, as some felt, madness) of architecture was added as another California oddity. In the early 1900s California as a place distinct from the rest of the U.S. became a major theme in its literature, arts, and architecture. California's drippingly sentimental cultivation of the Mission Revival in architecture, followed by its passionate, indeed almost religious, conversion to the Spanish Colonial Revival in the 1920s, were broad-scale efforts to make the contrast between the American East and Midwest as sharp and as startling as possible.

It could well be argued that the high point of California's stance as the land of the unique was directly tied to the emergence of California as Automobile-Land. In addition to providing the means of realizing suburbia, that greatest of American ideals, the automobile encouraged an entirely new response to how, on a day-to-day basis, we could experience our built or planted environment. California's mildness of climate, with the resulting ability to cheaply and quickly erect structures, encouraged a nonserious view of not only architecture, but symbolism and salesmanship as well. Why not make the process of selling and buying as lighthearted and enjoyable as aspects of the free living which California had made possible?

And if Californians were going to be fully committed to this "auto-mania" (as it was called in the teens), then why not cultivate a set of architectural images which would instantly catch the eye, and which we would continue to remember? Driving by or attending a motion picture showing in Los Angeles at Grauman's Chinese Theatre (Meyer and Holler, 1927) or at the Egyptian Theater (Meyer and Holler, 1922) or at the Mayan Theater (Morgan, Wells, and Clements, 1928) was not an experience easily forgotten. Equally, a run by a tire manufacturing company

posing as an Assyrian palace (Samson Tire and Rubber Co., Morgan, Walls, and Clements, 1929) was a far more effective way of pressing us to remember the product than a series of roadside billboards.

The introduction of the automobile made possible the linear, horizontal spread of Los Angeles with its resulting low density and low land values, and in the process it brought about the development of a wide range of auto-oriented, drive-in architecture. California, and Los Angeles in particular, did not originate auto-oriented signage and architecture, but its physical environment, its lifestyle, and its degree of commitment to the automobile made its fulfillment possible in the Southern California scene. As the New York–based editors of the *Architectural Forum* noted in an article, "Palaces of the Hot Doges," published in 1935, "... anything haywire is always most haywire in California." [2]

The quantity of spoken and written verbiage devoted to high art painting and sculpture published in our century has often led us to respond to their symbolic intent rather than their purely visual image. The truth is that the museum label, scholarly art historical slide presentation, or coffee table monograph on a major artist often seems greater than the object itself.

Except for a high art small elite, architecture has not yet experienced a similar wholesale transference of values from the world of symbolism. So far the middle-class audience has not been pressed first to read an explanation of a building and then go out and experience it. This is not to imply that direct and indirect symbolism does not exist in buildings, but rather that the visual language generally employed within our Western European architectural tradition has been a popular coinage generally understood by most members of society. In the twentieth century, the architectural language of the Colonial Revival, English Tudor, French Norman, or Classical Beaux Arts has been, through its historical allusions, direct and understandable. Equally, buildings which were clothed in the garb of the new, ranging from the Art Nouveau, to the Zig Zag (Art Deco) and Streamline Moderne, to the International Style (Modern) were addressed to a wide audience, ranging from the architectural elite to the middle class. In most instances these Period Revival or Modern buildings might well reveal layers of symbolic subtleties understood by only a few, but a knowledge of these subtleties was not necessary for a middle-class American to respond to the essential symbolism of each of these different images.

If we glance back to history and examine our European inheritance in architecture, we will find that the symbolic intent displayed by buildings can (with just a little squeezing here and there) be placed in several different pigeonholes. The largest of these compartments would accommodate the time-honored tradition of architectural borrowings or plagiarism from architecture's own past. The use of past architectural languages to comment on both the past and present is an overriding quality of the classical tradition of Greece and Rome itself. Equally, the direct and indirect borrowings experienced during the medieval period, and thence the Renaissance to the present moment, illustrate how

Opposite. **The Pup Cafe, 12728 Washington Boulevard, Culver City, California, 1929.** *Above.* **The Glacier, in the Angelus Mesa district of Los Angeles on Crenshaw Boulevard near Vernon Avenue, shown in context with its urban roadside environment, ca 1928.**

the European tradition of architectural borrowing has been its dominant, most consistent theme.

A second, much smaller pigeonhole should be provided for symbolic borrowings which lie outside the realm of traditional architectural language. These exterior borrowings range from the zoological and botanical forms to those taken from the idealized realm of geometry such as spheres and squares. The entrance to a garden grotto through the mouth of a river monster, a multistory dwelling built as an elephant, or a sphere as a house, and, in our century, an enlarged hot dog as fast-food restaurant are programatic devices meant to convey a set array of meanings. As with traditional architectural borrowings, the nonarchitectural images may well be resplendent with architectural meaning; still they were meant to be readable by those who were to experience and use them.

Finally, there is another category of architectural borrowings that should be housed in its own tiny pigeonhole: these are those employing either elements of traditional architecture vocabulary or nontraditional forms to convey meaning by indirection. In the English Picturesque Garden Tradition of the eighteenth century, the miniature classical temple, the exotic Islamic kiosk, or the ruins of a medieval castle played a game of double transference. We were not being asked to respond to them in a straightforward fashion as examples of conventional architectural imagery; rather, their intent was to comment on the present and its relation to the past.

In the twentieth century a hotel built as an Aztec temple, or an enlarged ice cream cone used to sell ice cream employ similar elements of indirect symbolism. While the English Picturesque Garden was limited in its audience to the gentry who could read its meaning, such was not the case with most nontraditional architectural imagery in the twentieth century.

Before looking into the history of our nontraditional architectural borrowings it would be well to see if we could catalogue them in some fashion. The word "programatic" could be suggested as a possible all-embracing term to describe this specified approach to architectural language. The vocabulary employed in these buildings hinged on a program organized to convey meaning not directly but by indirection. The program

Left. **Claude-Nicolas Ledoux's caretaker's house (1780s) in the form of a free-standing sphere.** *Right.* **Jean-Jacques Lequeu's schematic for a barn in the form of a cow (1700s).**

of intent and the visual means employed were integral with one another. The audience, then, was being asked to respond not to the artifact, but to the programatic utterance lying behind the form. In traditional architectural borrowings, by contrast, the means (style or fashion) employed had an existence in its own right, regardless of other meanings which might be ascribed to it.

Programatic borrowings of the past divided themselves into two basic sources—those emanating from the world of high art and those derived from low art. Within our European tradition the principal low art examples have been signs to advertise and sell services and merchandise. For the literate as well as an illiterate audience a hanging sign in the form of a boot was a far more effective way of letting us know that this was a shoe shop than using the written word. A sign in the symbolic form of the product was a well-used device not only in the Middle Ages, but also in ancient Rome, and it has continued as a mode of communication right down to the present.

Alongside this programatic, one-to-one symbolism has been another convention of employing signs which expressed the name of the establishment. An inn whose name was "The Head of the Horse" might well advertise its presence by a cutout, slightly sculptured sign in the form of a horse's head. In the nineteenth century the scale of these programatic signs was greatly increased. Large sculptured forms might surmount or be placed in front of a building, directly or indirectly indicating its usage. As a case in point in the 1890s the Eleventh Street Branch of the Grand Central market in Oakland, California, boasted a fully sculptured, brightly painted cow which was three times the size of a real cow.[3]

A second source from our European past came out of the high art world of architecture and landscape architecture. The villa gardens of Imperial Rome confronted their visitors with fountains and grottos often in the form of real and mythical animals, humans and plants. Topiary—the sculpting of vegetation in the forms of animals and other exotica—was another time-honored tradition. Pliny the Younger, writing of his own garden at Tusulan, speaks of trees "...cut into a variety of shapes."[4] The Roman tradition of topiary continued on through the Middle Ages, and it was utilized with renewed enthusiasm during the Renaissance. In the sixteenth century and later, the specific symbolic Roman use of garden structures in the form of fantastic humans and animals came once more into play. It crept into the urban environment where in the 1593 Palazzo Zuccari in Rome, visitors entered the Palazzo through the mouth of an anxiously awaiting monster.

High art's principal contribution to Programatic architecture occurred in the eighteenth century in the English Picturesque Garden tradition and in the work at the end of the century of the classical Visionary architects.[5] These architects pursued three versions of Programatic architecture. Their dominant commitment was to the world of geometry transformed—transformed in scale, and put to factual and symbolic usages. Claude-Nicolas Ledoux's often illustrated quarters for the rural caretakers of the 1780s, in the form of a free-standing sphere, disassociated from the landscape, is an example which immediately comes to mind. The single geometric form of the sphere, symbolic of geometry, could also be enshrouded with an overlay of other meanings. Etienne-Louis Boulée's memorial to Isaac Newton (1784) used the sphere to symbolize the Newtonian view of the universe, while Ledoux employed the sphere in his Plan for a Cemetery (1773–79) to evoke a sense of death and the underworld. These French, German, English, and American visionary architects employed a full package of programatic tricks to yank and pull us out of the world of everyday reality. Traditional architectural elements and parts of buildings were raised to a scale diverging from reality. Forms were borrowed from man's real or mythical past or from the faraway worlds of China, India, and the Near East. Buildings which borrowed entirely non-traditional architectural imagery included Ledoux's Woodcutter's House and Workshop (1773–79) in the form of a pyramidal stack of wood, Boulée's Cenotaph for a Warrior (undated), where we were confronted with a classical sarcophagus which has been blown up into a large building, and finally Jean-Jacques Lequeu's Barn in the Form of a Cow (undated).

The nineteenth century continued this high art tradition of Programatic architecture in only a marginal way. Certain pure geometric forms, such as the octagon, enjoyed great popularity, but the programatic exoticism of this form became so watered down in fact and symbolic content that most people of the time responded to it within its own advertised realm of supposed rationalism and utility. By the 1880s the exoticism of non-European architectural languages—Islamic, Chinese, and Japanese—had become so commonplace in the way they were used that they could only be marginally thought of as Programatic.

In contrast, the popular nineteenth-century scene provided a much stronger continuity between the distant past and our century. Signage—in scale, lavishness, and in sheer quantity—put the pre-1800 world to shame. Nowhere was this more true than in the United States, where by the end of the century immense thirty- to forty-foot billboards were erected in towns and cities. Anticipating the billboards was the convention of painting signs directly on the walls of buildings; it was in the latter half of the nineteenth century that this practice was expanded so that entire walls of commercial buildings and rural barns were transformed into giant advertising signs.

An important link in the upward and inward progress of Programatic buildings was a few structures in the form of elephants and other creatures, the most widely known being James F. Lafferty's come-on elephant "Lucy" built at South Atlantic City (Margate City) in 1881.[6] Lafferty's sixty-five-foot creation was modeled on the designs of the French architect Charles-François Ribart for a garden kiosk in the form of an elephant which were published in 1758. Ribart's creatures served as a symbol of the triumphs of the French crown; Lafferty's nineteenth-century elephant sold real estate.

Around the turn of the century there was an increase of Programatic buildings in amusement promenades of national and international expositions and in a growing number of amusement parks. The impact of these buildings tended to be somewhat different, for they existed in a noneveryday environment: their visual amusement or shock was minimal compared to what happens when these unfamiliar forms pop up in our everyday world.

During the twentieth century it was the introduction of the automobile which promoted a new wave of direct Programatic architecture. Not only did the coming of

Left. **The July 11, 1885 edition of** *Scientific American* **featured James F. Lafferty's schematics for the Colossal Elephant of Coney Island (1884).** *Right.* **Charles-François Ribart's garden kiosk in the form of an elephant (1758).**

the automobile encourage the Programatic, it could even participate in its spirit as in 1911 when the California Corrugated Culvert Company of San Francisco had its company car built in the form of a corrugated culvert, which by chance happened to have an engine and four wheels.[7] The usage of enlarged sculptured products to sell, which had begun in the nineteenth century, was raised both physically and symbolically to new heights in the first two decades of this century. In Indianapolis, a milk company constructed two fifty-two-foot-high milk bottles of glazed bricks, and other smaller-scale milk bottles, beer jugs, and wine bottles began to appear along America's developing systems of highways.[8] It was during the

elaborate sculptural program worked for the Nebraska State Capitol Building in Lincoln by Bertram Goodhue, the philosopher Hartley Burr Alexander, and the sculptor Lee Lawrie added the remote highfalutin reference to the past expected of a public building, but, because of its limited audience this approach could certainly not be used to sell an everyday product of American industry.[11] As a rule, the popular architectural sculpture of American Moderne generally assumed a more programatic approach. The four tympanum figures over the entrance to Los Angeles' black and gold Richfield building (Morgan, Walls, and Clements, 1928) symbolized Aviation, Postal Service, Industry, and Navigation—all of course powered by oil.[12] These classically inspired fig-

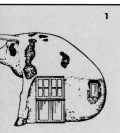 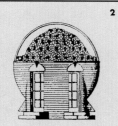 

1   2   3

① Barbeque Stand – Patent No. 90303
William H. Alston – San Antonio, Texas, 1933

② Building Patent – No. 77141
Warren E. Wolfe – Los Angeles, California, 1928

③ Refreshment Building – Patent No. 82865
Eugene L. Weaver – Los Angeles, California, 1930

next two decades, the 1920s and 1930s, that the many forms of Programatic architecture were firmly ensconced on the scene. Though there were examples built on the Continent and in England, it was the U.S., and especially the West Coast, which brought forth most of the examples.

The popular version of the modern, the Zigzag Moderne (Art Deco) of the twenties and of the early thirties, introduced Programatic elements into its buildings. In the gem of the Moderne—the Chrysler building in New York (1930)—the architect William Van Alen established a Programatic decorative program of "...glorifying American mechanical genius and incidentally Mr. Chrysler's output of cars, trucks, and boats."[9] Radiator caps and emblems were used for flagpole sockets and "...on the thirteenth story, the brick-work wheels revolved under horizontal mudguards...."[10] In Los Angeles, the Sunset Towers, one of the city's major contributions to the Moderne (Leland A. Bryant, 1929–31), helps us to locate the enclosed parking garage by placing terra cotta automobile fronts below and above the windows.

The exponents of the Moderne maneuvered themselves even closer to the pretenses of high art in their frequent use of programatic sculpture. Sculpture depicting specific historic individuals from classical and nonclassical sources was a favored device of the European and American Beaux Arts tradition from the 1890s through the 1930s. But such figures demanded some degree of humanistic erudition so that the audience could fully comprehend what was supposedly symbolized. The

ures were made understandable (it was hoped) by adding wings and a propeller to the figure of Aviation, and by attaching similar easily recognizable appendages to the other three figures.

The play between innuendoes of high art and direct programatic art was a theme which occurred with moderate frequency in roadside advertising of the 1920s. The serious-minded lamented what they saw happening to the roadside. With the completion of an extensive portion of the national highway system by the early 1930s the advantages of regional and national repetitive highway signage came into the picture. The most extravagant of these were the sequential Burma Shave signs with their quizzical utterances luring the driver to the final Burma Shave sign, and sign notices throughout the upper Midwest leading up to Wall's Drug Store in Wall, South Dakota. The image of the Burma Shave signage was fitting for a national product while the Wall's Drug Store signs had an appropriate fallen-down Western look.

The California architect Robert H. Orr noted that the way things were going, "...our highways, byways, and street corners will be lined with sculptural monuments revealing those strewn along the 'Holy Way' to the ancient Tombs of the Mings."[13] What Orr was referring to were three-dimensional sculptural advertising signs usually consisting of a high base which bore the written message, and sculptural horses and riders, bulls, or racing cars placed on top. In some instances there was an understandable relationship between the sculpture above and whatever it advertised, as the figure of the bull helped name Ye Bull Pen Inn in Los

Angeles, or a depiction of Barney Oldfield and his racing car helped sell Richfield gasoline. In other instances, "famous" statuary was taken from the world of high art with seemingly no direct connection (other than the prestige of "Art") between the sculpted figure and the advertising product. The inventiveness of Programatic signage was especially evident in the 1930s. In 1931, the Coca-Cola Company used real-life female models to sit under make-believe palm trees to enjoy the "pause that refreshes."[14] The play between that which is and that which is not was frequently employed in large billboard signage when real objects occurred within an illusionary painted sign. The General Sign Company of Oakland placed a coupe

magazines (especially *The National Geographic* for the American middle-class audience) the world architectural scene was just waiting to be grabbed up. The rash of eighteenth- and nineteenth-century non-European borrowings was continued, although the context was meant to be more jarring, so that their indirect message could be more favorably conveyed. Egypt, Babylon, Assyria, Japan, China, and Hindu and Islamic India provided vocabularies for anything ranging from the interior of restaurants to motion picture theaters. Added to these older borrowings was a new group of "primitive images" derived from the Pacific world of Melanesia and Polynesia, the pre-European pueblos of the American Southwest, the teepees of

Refreshment Stand – Patent No. 93665 ④
Warren Lee – Los Angeles, California, 1934

Booth Patent – No. 107561 ⑤
Daniel G. Terrie – Rockville Centre, New York

Igloo Patent – No. 81860 ⑥
John Henry Whitington – Los Angeles, California, 1928

from the Howard Motor Company within a tropical island setting complete with a sunset, and on the roadside outside of Milwaukee, there was a real yellow-and-silver airplane, apparently crashing into the ground. This eye-catcher let the passing motorist know it was only a twenty-minute drive to a Schuster's Department Store.[15] A subtle, complex interchange between the real and the illusionary occurred in a large sign in Indianapolis, where a gigantic make-believe mirror enlarged a moving sequence of views of the individual shops located in the Circle Tower Shopping Center. In this instance the signage with its movement accentuated by changing colored lights existed as an intermediator between the potential customer and the actual passage into the individual shops.[16]

Another twentieth-century link with the Programatic architecture of the past is to be found in the use of architectural imagery which was either exotic (the faraway or distant past), or was a perversion of some past European architectural mode. Forms which we would loosely label as "medieval" were a favorite imagery of the 1920s. But this medieval imagery was meant to be read through our remembrances of the fairy-tale world of Hansel and Gretel.[17] These little witches' cottages—which might serve as real estate offices, service stations, or fast food restaurants—play an intriguing game with scale and other make-believe elements. They are, in fact, dollhouses enlarged, but kept at distances from the world of traditional imagery.

The range of non-European traditional imagery utilized during the twenties reveals that through popular

the Plains Indians, and the Pre-Columbian architecture of the Maya, the Zapotec, and the Aztec of Mexico and Central America.

During the thirties these exotic borrowings were joined and almost overwhelmed by the imagery of the Streamline Moderne. The Streamline Moderne, as a popular architectural system of imagery, seized the element of speed—epitomized in the aerodynamic design of the airplane—and applied it to the full range of designed products, including signage and large and small buildings. Even signs were caught up in the Streamline urge: "...if outdoor advertising is to keep its foremost place among advertising mediums it must keep its foremost place in design, too, along with motor cars and airplanes and railroad trains."[18] That which distinguishes the Streamline Moderne has to do with how the audience was asked to respond to the building. In the case of a Streamline Moderne building the audience was expected to see it as architecture which had been clothed in a modern garb. Programatic Streamline Moderne buildings exist in the form, for example, of a streamlined train as a diner, a streamlined boat as a restaurant, or a streamlined automobile as a service station.[19] By the end of the 1930s the Streamline Moderne image, with its hint at what glories lay in store for us in the future, had almost entirely supplanted the older languages of Programatic architecture.

An illustration of how the twenties could be tied to the thirties and how the past could be linked to the future can be seen in the many fast-food hamburger shops in the form of streamlined castles. The single corner

tower used for the chain of White Tower hamburger shops was all that was needed to suggest that it was medieval.[20] The Wichita-based White Castle buildings played off the hygienic quality of white porcelain panels against crenelated parapet and tower, while the Tulsa-based Silver Castle chain ended up with a totally streamlined box which retained its allegiance to the medieval past solely through its name and logo.[21]

Turning our attention specifically to California's Programatic architecture of the twenties and thirties, it is of interest to note that these Programatic forms came onto the scene late in the 1920s and more of them were built during the opening years of the Great Depression than before. Though there were examples before 1928, their high point was between 1928 and 1934. This is borne out not only by examples which were constructed but by the numerous unbuilt examples for which patents were issued.[22] The ingenuity of American designers is pointedly and delightfully revealed in the array of "impossible" visual images which they patented. What was built in California and elsewhere in the country reveals only the tip of the iceberg in terms of America's faith in the Programatic to sell services and products. Lunch pails, jugs, teapots and cups, locks and keys, corncobs, milk bottles, ice cream cones and freezers, birthday cakes, icebergs, soup bowls, oranges, hot dogs, and tamales were joined by dogs, pigs, and dancing girls as constructions. There also were the machine themes applied to the buildings: airplanes, ships, automobiles, and even spark plugs and light bulbs.

If we apply our earlier categories to these examples, buildings and signs generally fall into two basic groups—those whose imagery directly conveys what was being sold, and those which employed a wide variety of indirect messages to advertise. All of the Programatic structures, whether a tamale stand built in the form of a tamale, or an airplane built as a service station, were created to be eye-catchers: they were meant to startle, shock, and amuse. Humor was an essential element in the audience's response to these structures. Even the streamlined passenger car as a diner, with its allusions to the future, was meant to convey a sort of lighthearted Buck Rogers excursion.

Direct Programatic architecture—the structure as a sign of what it was selling—succeeded because of the simplicity of its symbolism, whereas indirect Programatic architecture entailed degrees of meaning which, one suspects, had the potential of holding the audience's attention for a longer period of time. An enlarged hot dog which sold hot dogs exemplifies a first step in the process of injecting indirect meaning into the architectural vocabulary. An iceberg to sell cold soft drinks and ice cream or a teapot or coffeepot built as a restaurant suggests that this is a place where food and drink may be obtained. A service station in the shape of an airplane asks that the audience symbolically connect two machines with the selling and consuming of energy-producing products.

All of these buildings somehow manage to maintain connections between the form of the structure and what is being advertised, but such is not the case for a wide variety of exotic languages which often occurs in Programatic architecture. An owl enlarged to a small building, which housed an ice cream stand, reveals no connection between the product and the form of the building. Perhaps, it might be suggested, there is linkage to be found in the childhood world of fairy tales,

reinforced in the twenties and thirties by the dream world of the Hollywood motion picture. The architectural garb provided in Los Angeles by Grauman's Chinese Theatre, the Egyptian Theater, and the Mayan Theater was openly employed to carry the theater-goer into an intermediary noneveryday world, and thence into the visual mythology of the film. The far distant lands of the Egyptians, of the Mayans, and the Chinese were, by the mid-twenties, a more effective device to carry the audience into the film than the earlier usage of the sumptuous Beaux Arts baroque.

The most prevalent building types associated with Programatic architecture were those associated with the automobile and drive-in architecture. Here the need for quick identification at a reasonable speed and distance meant that a building which could catch the eye could or should draw in customers. In writing about Pasadena's well-known Mother Goose Pantry (1929), which was built as a great shoe, a writer noted that "…[Foothill] Boulevard is lined with wayside places of various types and designs for miles. Every one of these is forgotten, however, save the famous Mother Goose Pantry."[23]

A theme which enjoyed great popularity throughout the U.S. was that of the frontier log cabin. One of the earliest of these in California was the ca 1911 Old Log Cabin refreshment stand in San Diego. Numerous variations on this theme were carried out in California in the 1920s and 1930s, including buildings in the form of a single tree trunk. In 1930 the log cabin was seized upon as an architectural style for a chain of small fast-food restaurants, the White Log taverns. The first of these was built in Oakland, and by 1937 there were sixty-two of these fast-food restaurants located through-

out California.[24] The White Log Taverns, with their frames of steel sheathed in concrete logs, played off two sets of images—that of log cabin and that of the American Colonial Style. For a national image, this added up to the best of two worlds. Another California example of the virtues of the American home and the frontier was The Big Fireplace restaurant in Los Angeles (1927), which greeted its customers with two giant-scale exterior fireplaces augmented by a pattern of ever-changing red lights. The parking lot and the street had become one great big living room.[25]

More indicative of the California scene, and especially of Southern California, was the occurrence of Hansel and Gretel architecture. The first of these buildings on the Los Angeles scene was designed by Harry Oliver, who was a set designer for Metro-Goldwyn-Mayer Studios. In 1921 he designed the studio offices for Irvin C. Willat Productions in Culver City. "We have tried," noted Irvin C. Willat, "to reproduce a tumble-down structure of two centuries ago, but which will be equipped with the most modern office appurtenances."[26] The reason for this cultivated architectural exoticism was no different than that for a drive-in restaurant. A 1921 newspaper article of the time reported, "It is said that this structure has occasioned more comments from passing motorists than any building being erected in Los Angeles in recent months."[27]

Within a year Oliver went on to design the first Van de Kamp's Bakery's famous shingle-covered windmills,

Opposite. **The Old Log Cabin, University Avenue, San Diego, ca 1911.** *Above.* **The Freezer, painted its original brown color, Fourth Street and North Western Avenue, Los Angeles, 1927.**

and the Tam o' Shanter Restaurant located on Los Feliz near Griffith Park.[28] The Tam o' Shanter restaurant was supposedly California's first drive-in restaurant, and it was the first of the Los Angeles drive-ins to consciously cultivate the world of Alice in Wonderland.[29] Its fairy-tale atmosphere was openly connected at the time to Hollywood: "…The Tam o' Shanter Restaurant is the product of movie town architecture efficiently applied."[30]

In the late twenties and early thirties, movieland versions of Hansel and Gretel cottages were built throughout the West Los Angeles area, many of which were designed by the productive and professionally respected firm of Pier-

marginal establishments which employed the Pueblo Revival, the Moorish or Islamic Revival, and the Pre-Columbian of Mexico and Central America. Gay's Lion Farm (1926) in El Monte and, above all, the impossible Cliff Dwellers cafe on Beverly Boulevard (1927) illustrate how a non-European architectural image could be pulled into the realm of the Programatic. Equally strained in its relationship to the traditional were a wide array of Islamic-inspired designs: the Calmos #1 Service Station (1925) on Hollywood Boulevard with its domed mosque-like station which is accompanied by two minarets, and Roland E. Coate's Calpet Service Station (1928) on Wilshire Boulevard where the final touch was the female Moorish attendants who serviced

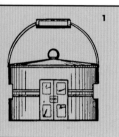 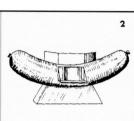 

1. Building Design – Patent No. 94787
   Andrew J. Stevens – Kansas City, Missouri, 1934

2. Vending Stand – Patent No. 78662
   Anthony Soucie – Oakland, California, 1928

3. Chili Booth – Patent No. 83335
   Volney A. McLaren – Wichita, Kansas 1929

pont and Walter S. Davis. Robert H. Derrah, who is best remembered for his Coca-Cola Company building in the form of a streamlined ocean liner, employed the Alice in Wonderland theme for his Continental Villa, which formed a segment of his 1936 Cross Roads of the World on Sunset.[31] Half-timbered medievalism continued on into the post–World War II years, but these later examples establish their relationship to the traditional world of architectural imagery, rather than to the storybook world of Alice or Hansel and Gretel.

In the East, South, and Midwest, the Colonial was by far the favored image for a wide variety of small roadside commercial buildings, ranging from service stations to restaurants. In California the imagery of the Colonial was occasionally used, as in Fatty Arbuckle's Plantation Cafe of 1926 on Washington Boulevard. In this case, it was the signage on the roof and the signing on the long mound of turf which pull the structure and its setting out of the normal world of architecture. That this perversion of the past has not left us is readily apparent in the 1960 Pacific Savings (now California Federal Savings) designed by Rick Farver Associates, where the full-blown vestige of George Washington's Mount Vernon has been moved from the shores of the Potomac to a safe site overlooking the Hollywood Freeway.

More instances of California's Mission, Hispanic, and Mediterranean imagery used for small-scale commercial purposes tended to be rather straight-forward interpretations of one or another of these modes. Just off the path of traditional architecture were those

your Packard or Franklin. The Islamic theme was employed for King's Tropical Inn on Washington Boulevard (1926), which somehow sought to connect its specialty chicken dinners with the exotic world of Africa and the Near East. In the thirties the imagery of the Land of the Arabian Knights encouraged an Iranian mosque for the Beverly Theatre (1930–31) and for the extensive offices of the Girard Real Estate Development (1928) on Ventura Boulevard.

While the downtown Mayan Theater was locally the most widely known of Los Angeles' pre-Columbian exercises, the most extensively written about was Robert Stacy-Judd's Aztec Hotel (1926) in Monrovia.[32] The delightful and at times humorously mad maneuvering of historic images can be seen if we compare the Oriental theme of the Mandarin Market (1929–30) on Vine and Grauman's Chinese Theatre, or the Egyptian assertions of Glendale's Egyptian Village Cafe (1924) and the Egyptian Theater in Hollywood.

A recurring theme in the eighteenth-century architecture was the return of the primitive, symbolized by the wood and thatched hut. Primitive or indigenous architecture was also played upon as a theme in Programatic architecture of the twenties and later. These images ranged from colorful Arab tents used to sell tropical fruits and juices, to thatched restaurants offering South Seas cuisine. The theme with the widest popular appeal was the Plains Indian teepee. Here was a form which was closely tied to the romance of the West. To spend a night in a teepee motel or have one's car serviced at a teepee village was a marvelous way to imply a connection between the nomadic Plains Indians, the westward movement of covered wagons, and the automobile and the open highway.

Los Angeles' gift to America of buildings and signage represents a mixed-up world of myth and fact. Promotional trade, popular and professional publications obviously delighted in illustrating Los Angeles roadside buildings in the form of oranges, jugs, and flowerpots. Photographs of these Programatic buildings not only presented startling visual objects to their readers, but there was always the implication that the buildings illustrated were typical of the scene.[33] As artifacts of the roadside scene these Programatic buildings often lack

repeated theme was the building in the form of a milk bottle, but other exotica—oranges, artichokes, and pumpkins—entered the scene.

The heyday of California's Programatic buildings occurred during the ten-year period from 1925 through 1934. It was in these years that the most famous of the California examples were built: the Hoot Hoot I Scream building (1925); the Brown Derby restaurant (1926); the Sphinx Realty building (1927); the Igloo building (1928); the Tamale building (1928); the Mother Goose Pantry restaurant (1929); the Zep Diner building (1930); the Toed Inn stand (1931); and the Pig Cafe (1934). While there were a few buildings

Vending Structure – Patent No. 95314 **4**
Alfred H. Burks – Dayton, Ohio

Building – Patent No. 86683 **5**
Sadie O'Neil – Seattle, Washington, 1931

Resort Building – Patent No. 105823 **6**
Herman E. Olson – Seattle, Washington, 1937

the usual documentation associated with larger, more conventional, buildings. It is unlikely that we will ever know just how many of them were actually built. Altogether there were probably less than seventy-five Programatic buildings built in Southern California. What strikes one in looking through the published illustrations of these buildings is that only a small handful—less than a dozen—were illustrated over and over again. Generally the buildings which were repeatedly published were the most flamboyant, though one often has a sneaky suspicion that these were the Programatic buildings which by chance happened to have been photographed. While the Hoot Hoot I Scream stand in the form of an owl was located on Long Beach Boulevard, this was not a street which would normally be traveled by the casual visitor to Los Angeles. Thus the picture represented at the time and later that Los Angeles and Southern California highways and streets were lined by hundreds of Programatic buildings was simply not true.

The chronological history of Programatic buildings in California closely follows the pattern already mentioned in the discussion of traditional architectural imagery. One of the earliest examples was Albert Kenney's 1903–04 restaurant ship "Cabrillo" and Venetian Garden, which was situated on the Venice Pier.[34] This make-believe ship on piles pretended at one moment to be a Spanish galleon; at the next it was a fragment of a Venetian palace. By 1920, Kenny's ship "Cabrillo" was joined by a small scattering of buildings and three-dimensional signs situated in both Northern and Southern California. An often

constructed after 1935—such as Cobb's Chicken House at the 1939 San Francisco World Fair—which directly continued this earlier tradition, later Programatic transformations looked almost exclusively to the Streamlined Moderne image of the transportation machine for sources. In Los Angeles, Robert H. Derrah's streamlined ocean liner for the Coca-Cola Building (1936) was the grandest example, while all that was needed was a set of tracks for the streamlined train engine of Alice Faye's Club Car Restaurant (1941) to streak off into the night.[35] The image of the airplane, as the most advanced transportation machine, was employed for service stations, and in 1939 Charlie Le Maire, the Los Angeles restaurateur, patented the Skyline Diner, which was in the form of a Norman Bel Geddes double-decked streamlined airplane.[36] The Dark Room (1938) on Wilshire moves us programatically into the objects sold by employing a streamlined image of a camera as its storefront.

When building activities resumed in California in 1945 after the war, there was almost a complete absence of Programatic buildings. The often illustrated Tail o' the Pup on La Cienega Boulevard was built or refurbished in 1946, the Wigwam Village in Rialto was built in 1955, along with a few others—just enough examples to indicate that, although low keyed, the tradition was not dead.[37] The image of the doughnut as a symbol for fast food entered the California scene in 1954 with The Big Do-Nut chain, and numerous variations were built like The Do-Nut Hole (1958) in the City of Industry. In more recent years the older Programatic buildings have been joined by the Shutterbug (1977) in

Westminster, and by the giant Caterpillar as a tractor salesroom in Turlock (1978).[38] There was, though, no break in California's usage of Programatic signage between the pre– and post–World War II years. The early Programatic signage of a wide-eyed puppy dog which looks down at us from atop Barkies Sandwich Shops (1930–31) was augmented in the Post-War period by the giant woman's leg which lets us know that this is indeed Sanderson's Stockings (1948), and by the red-and-white Santa Claus (1950) that announces this is the town of Santa Claus, California.

Variations on this form of architectural signage were large-scale billboards and entire building facades which formed sculptured signs. Clifton's Cafeteria on Olive Street in downtown Los Angeles (1931) with its water-falls, geysers, and tropical foliage was matched, if not surpassed, by the scene of romping and frolicking pigs which in painted and sculpted forms crawl over the walls and buildings of Farmer John's Meat Packing Plant in Vernon.[39]

The approach taken to language in these Programatic buildings or in signage ran the gamut between direct commentary and the exotic. The building in the form of the product sold—a tamale, orange, or lemon—is as obvious as one could ask. The next step of symbolism plays on the theme of the container or mechanism used in the production of the product: the flowerpot as a nursery or flower store, a cream can to sell dairy products, or a hand-cranked freezer to dispense ice cream products. A third set of symbols goes one step further by hinting at some quality associated with the product: an igloo and iceberg to sell cold drinks and ice cream, or a coffeepot to advise the viewer that this is a restaurant.

Then there are those buildings that comment on their names—The Brown Derby, The Toed Inn, or The Pig Cafe. There is often an essential need for the Progra-matic form of the building to be accompanied in this case by written signage so that the potential customer can tie the form and name together. Behind this play between the form and the written word is another ele-ment of attraction as to the whys and wherefores of the name itself. The shoe as a building for Pasadena's Mother Goose Pantry Restaurant is meant to pull us directly back into childhood.

But what levels of humorous meanings lie behind such themes as the Round House Cafe (1927), with its train engine plunging out toward us, or the World War I theme of a crashed airplane and sandbagged trenches of The Dugout (1927) in Montebello? The child's world of the fairy tale certainly lies behind The Mush-rooms Restaurant (1928) in Burbank, and Pumpkin Palace restaurant (1927) in Burbank, but other themes like the walled and guarded Jail Cafe (1926) must somehow appeal to other parts of our sensibilities. The suggestion that there should be a give-and-take between the real, everyday world and some other world was the overriding theme of California's Programatic excursion into the Streamline transportation machine. In the instances of streamlined ships, trains, and air-planes of the late thirties and early forties we are asked

Above. **The impact of programmatic buildings along the emerging cityscape is apparent in this view of the Umbrella Gas Station, 830 South La Brea Avenue, Los Angeles, ca 1928.** *Opposite.* **In true roadside fashion, the Orange Inn (ca 1927), a refreshment stand and outdoor market on Foothill Boulevard in Arcadia, attracts tourists destined for Los Angeles with an attention-getting, giant orange.**

to hop, skip, and jump back and forth between the then-existing works of technology, the world of Buck Rogers and Flash Gordon, and the machine-dominated futurism of the twenty-first century.

Programatic architecture and signage were almost universally condemned by America's upper middle class, professional planners, and the high art world. The first two groups felt (and quite rightly so) that Programatic structures, like billboards and roadside architecture in general, would destroy the City Beautiful sense of order in an urban environment, as well as the sylvan quality of suburbia. They were uncomfortable with the blatant commercialism these structures implied. The proponents of high art were afraid that the frequent use of sculpture in this fashion would debase the original, asking "Will they not eventually make sculpture ... so commonplace that the real object of art cannot, except by those especially trained, be disassociated from the commonplace and cause a decadency far-reaching in its effect and influence?"[40] In a way, of course, this is just what happened. Bit by bit the high art world of Cubism, Futurism, and, above all, Dadaism, Surrealism, and Pop has so mixed, transformed, and been transformed, that today a high arter and a good bourgeois will respond with equal ardor to those few remaining vestiges of our Programatic near-past.

It was the foremost of America's architectural historians, Henry Russell Hitchcock, who as early as 1936 noted that, "The combination of strict functionalism and bold symbolism in the best roadside stands provides, perhaps, the most encouraging sign for the architecture of the mid-twentieth century."[41]

This affirmative response went basically unheeded and did not reappear until the 1950s in the pages of *Landscape*, which was founded and edited by J. Brickerhoff Jackson. Jackson, and the writers he assembled in the pages of *Landscape*, asked us to reassess the whole of our commercial vernacular including the highway and the commercial strip.[42] The imperative which Hitchcock had in mind for Programatic architecture finally arrived in the mid-sixties though the publication of Robert Venturi's volume, *Complexity and Contradiction in Architecture*, and in the buildings which he and his associates design.[43] Venturi's Duck (Martin H. Maurer's Roadside Stand near Riverhead, Long Island, 1933), symbolizing buildings as signs, brought the whole of Programatic buildings back into high-art respectability.[44] Since the early seventies the Programatic tradition of borrowing from architectural imagery itself and from outside of it has returned with a fervor. In California it seems almost to be a repeat of what occurred in the relationship of the use of programatic forms within the eighteenth-century English Picturesque Garden tradition and the later occurrence of "real" Progamatic buildings. In the 1950s, California began to experience a rash of miniature golf courses resplendent with a wonderful array of toy-sized buildings; by the mid-seventies they began to be supplemented by "real" buildings. Whether the rich treasure trove of California's Programatic buildings will provide a similar inspiration for the present remains to be seen. One hopes it will.

David Gebhard
Director, University of California Art Museum
Santa Barbara, California

Above. The Twin Inns in Carlsbad, California (1924), drew travellers to their roadside restaurant with an advertising sculpture suggesting chicken dinners. *Opposite page: Top*. The Betsy Ann ice cream outlet in Hollywood, ca 1928. *Bottom*. Two large-scale roadside sculptures announce to motorists Petaluma's claim of chicken- and egg-producing capital of the world.

CHAPTER 1

CALIFORNIA CRAZY

California has never lacked superlatives. The Golden State's claim as host to the largest concentration of bizarre and odd-shaped buildings is just another feather in the cap of a state whose reputation was built on towns that called themselves the "artichoke capital of the world" or "home to the world's largest chinchilla farm." While Southern California contained a large amount of offbeat buildings, the rest of the state enjoyed a healthy sampling of architectural anomalies as well. Given the freewheeling nature of California, its perceived lack of history, wealth of affordable land, and anything-goes attitude, it is easy to see why the state and climate were perfect for embracing these buildings.

Reinforced by Chamber of Commerce boosters, railroad companies, and real estate promoters, California quickly transformed itself by a series of land booms in the latter part of the nineteenth century that continued through to the first part of the twentieth. These land booms brought a tremendous influx of new arrivals to the state, who borrowed or brought their architectural heritages with them. The lack of an architectural tradition and the motivation by transplants to the Golden State to start fresh and experiment brought an eclectic vision to the area.

Before the automobile became a fixture on the landscape and accelerated the construction of roadside architecture, Californians were treated to a more sedate assortment of architectural aberrations. Various revivals of historic periods were popular in commercial ventures, especially when the Mission Style became fashionable in the 1880s. Transit stations, stores, and schools borrowed elements of a romantic mission past, thereby rein-

forcing once again the illusion of a California that never was. In the early part of the twentieth century, the Arts and Crafts movement provided a touch of Asian flavor. Craftsman bungalows featured the best examples of this influence and the pagoda-like homes that lined many a new suburban tract were a striking contrast to the California landscape.

During this same time period in Southern California, where no tradition impeded them, developers experimented with a variety of architectural styles. In 1912, the *Los Angeles Times* made note of this

Above. The facade of Tehuantepec, an amusement attraction on the Zone, Panama Pacific International Exposition, San Francisco, 1915. *Left, top.* Bungalows with exotic overtones line the streets of a developing Los Angeles, ca 1920. *Left, bottom.* A bungalow catalogue provided the inspiration for many unusual forms of domestic imagery, ca 1920. *Opposite page:* (1) A panorama of Venice, ca 1910, showing the Ship restaurant on the Venice pier. (2) The volcano entrance to the Grand Canyon Electric Railroad, a thrill ride in Ocean Park, ca 1911. (3) The Ship Cafe. (4) The Midway Plaisance in Venice evoked an exotic presence on the flatlands of Los Angeles, ca 1906. (5) The wildly fanciful entrance to Dragon Gorge, a roller coaster on the Fraser Pier, Ocean Park, ca 1911. (6) Devils Gorge at the White City Amusement Park in Chicago extended credence to the influence of amusement architecture on programmatic buildings.

Dragon Gorge,
Ocean Park, Cal.

White City Amusement Park,
Devils Gorge, 63d Str. and
So. Park Ave., Chicago.

experimental climate in describing the construction of a downtown apartment building that claimed to be the first to adapt early Aztec architecture to modern structural designing:

"Los Angeles is noted for the diversity of architecture entering the planning of its buildings, the types of design here being almost as cosmopolitan as the population. Every type of architecture prevailing in the Mediterranean countries of Europe has been copied and adapted. The Englishman has brought here the sturdy lines of the British buildings. The chateau in its many forms has suited the ideas of many. The charming Swiss chalet has been modified to suit local requirements and has become one of the most popular of all styles. The Mission, California's own architecture, is to be encountered at every turn. The bungalow has here taken on an individuality and charm that has won for the Southland types a

Above. Attractions in the "Zone" at the 1915 Panama Pacific Exposition in San Francisco inspired future programmatic building in California. *Right.* The unusual begins to sprout along California roadsides. Sphinx head, location and date unknown. *Opposite page: Top.* An early entry defining exotic Los Angeles, the Shrine Auditorium, ca 1920. *Middle.* The Krotona complex above Hollywood brought intonations of the mysterious East to the film capital, ca 1912. *Bottom.* The Theosophists' commune in Point Loma near San Diego, ca 1900.

worldwide reputation. Every Eastern American type has been introduced here.

"That the architecture of the prehistoric civilizations of North America has never been copied by the builders has occasioned comment at times from foreign visitors to this country. In Mexico and Central America especially the races found by the first white conqueror had developed not only a high degree of structural ingenuity, but a real sense of the artistic. It may be urged in their favor, too, that they were not copying from any classics of still more ancient days as were Europeans of the same period, and that their work was truly original."

When Abbott Kinney created his visionary development of Venice, California between 1904–06 on the marshlands of suburban Los Angeles, he was part of a pioneering effort that transformed Southern California from a vast agricultural plain to a land of fantasy and illusion. By importing the imagery of Venice, Italy for a cultural center and seaside resort, he helped set the tone for a free-spirited architectural atmosphere. Principal buildings of the resort followed Venetian lines while other attractions infused the area with the exotic. Gondolas glided along a grid of canals, camels paraded the streets giving visitors rides, and an early midway contained reproductions of the streets of Cairo and Tokyo. The Ship Cafe (1905) was one of the earliest of the faux buildings constructed on the Venice Pier. Built on the side of the

wharf extending over the ocean, it gave the illusion of resting on the water when in fact no part actually touched the ocean. The Ship Cafe's popularity reigned for several decades and peaked when the early Hollywood movie colony frequented it as a Prohibition hangout.

In a Venice amusement park that evolved out of the resort several years later, many buildings featured facades of fantastic proportions. Spilling out of the amusement zone and onto the boardwalk was the Venice Scenic Railway (1910), which was encased in a stucco mountain range with oversized deer clinging to the precipices. In the adjacent amusement zones of Ocean Park, massive stucco monsters flanked a thrill ride called Dragons Gorge (1911), a mountain rose from the Grand Canyon Scenic Railway (1911), and the Ocean Park bathhouse (1905) on the boardwalk was a maze of minarets and onion domes. For visitors as well as local residents, it was a giddy architectural

fantasy come true and another affirmation of California's animated architecture. As an architectural bridge, Venice provided the subtle inspiration for things to come.

The amusement zone at the 1915 Panama Pacific Exposition in San Francisco was also a showcase of whimsical structures that would clearly influence many of the oddball buildings that would be built in the forthcoming decade. "Captain, the Educated Horse" was an attraction that had a two-story stucco horse as an entry. Farther along the midway, a gigantic Uncle Sam bent over fairgoers while holding the fob to a giant watch that dangled over the Souvenir Watch Palace. A 120-foot gilded Buddha dominated the Japan Beautiful Pavilion, while three-story ostriches served as portals to the Ostrich Farm. The enormous Bowls of Joy were replicas of roly-poly toys that dwarfed the patrons standing in line for one of the Exposition's more dangerous thrill rides. Oversized jack-in-the-boxes,

colossal elephant heads, huge sculpted angels, and superscaled telephones and typewriters could be found scattered throughout the Zone and exposition pavilions. A fantasy secure behind fair walls, the buildings nonetheless had an impact on the public, as evidenced by the throngs that were drawn to the amusement zone. These structures would become a key visual language to a broader audience once outside the confines of an enclosed environment. This became apparent when Exposition visitor and Hollywood film director D. W. Griffith invited some of the sculptors to Hollywood where he had them construct the massive Babylonian sets for the film *Intolerance*, thus providing a transition from exposition to Hollywood studio, and ultimately, to the California roadside.

As the automobile gained momentum in the pre–World War I era, an eclectic mix of architectural styles continued to pop up along the roadside and in urban areas. These structures presaged more impossible structures to come, and most were replications of historical styles. These period revivals were often adaptations of European, Spanish, or Mediterranean architecture. For example, the Shrine Auditorium (1920–26) near downtown

Los Angeles employed the exotic imagery of the Middle East in one of its first auditoriums. In San Diego, the Old Log Cabin (1911), an early roadside refreshment stand, played with the idea of a rustic frontier past complete with an interior that exuded a pioneer atmosphere while dispensing soft drinks. The large Los Baños bathhouse in downtown San Diego was constructed in flamboyant Mission Style, while in nearby La Jolla, Anna Held, an eccentric and free-spirited artist, created an ark-shaped home as part of the Green Dragon Colony, an early twentieth century collection of cottages on the side of a hill. In Point Loma, across the San Diego Bay, an emerging Utopian commune, the Theosophists, constructed a Greek temple overlooking the ocean as well as a series of quasi-Asian buildings topped with onion-shaped domes of purple and aquamarine glass. Leslie Brand, a financier and a developer of Glendale, a Los Angeles suburb, created a mansion he named El Miradero (1902–04) on one

Above. **Atop a hill in the center of Hollywood, a magnificent replica of a Japanese temple showcased the Asian antiques of importers Adolph and Eugene Bernheimer, ca 1914.** *Opposite.* **"Sans Souci," the residence of Hollywood developer A. G. Schlosser at Franklin and Argyle Avenues, ca 1909.**

thousand acres of prime foothill land. "Saracenic" in style, it was inspired by the East Indian Pavilion of the 1893 Columbian Exposition in Chicago.

While many of these types of architectural styles and amusement parks were not exclusive to California, their confluence and impact on an emerging landscape was a striking contrast to companion structures and amusement zones in the other parts of the United States. It was becoming clear that California was slowly becoming crazier.

Hollywood, which was to become a magnet for architectural illusions, further enhanced the reputation for offbeat architecture even before the movies arrived. Real estate developer and retired doctor A. G. Schlosser built his fantasy mansion Glengarry Castle in the foothills at Franklin and Argyle in 1909. A mad collection of various castle-like elements, it was described as a "pretentious mansion with artistic decorations of the Louis 15th and Flemish periods created by Italian and German artists of note." Later it was joined by his Sans Souci Castle across the street, which was another bizarre house with overtones of baronial English

and German Rhine castles. It doubled as the Kaiser's house when filmmaker Mack Sennett featured the exterior in an antiwar propaganda film.

On the crest of a nearby hill, an equally out-of-place Japanese palace was built in 1914 by millionaire silk trader Adolph Bernheimer and his brother Eugene. The residence and surrounding gardens, which cascaded down the hillside, were visible from most points in Hollywood. A showplace of imported Oriental antiques, dense, garish interiors, and gardens sprinkled with fountains and pagodas, it drew visitors from around the world, thereby advancing the image of Southern California as a unique and unusual place.

California's position as a magnet for nonconformist beliefs further enhanced the construction of buildings in Hollywood. Several structures were built in conjunction with new philosophies and religions brought to the area. Krotona, a branch of the Adyar Theosophists, set up shop in 1912 in Hollywood and created a mosque-like temple complex and grounds in the foothills above the commercial district. Later, branches of the Self

Realization Fellowship would appear on Sunset Boulevard as well as farther down the coast in Encinitas, with both locations having buildings of Middle Eastern design. Outside of Southern California, numerous buildings of a similar style appeared up and down the coast. Among them, the Rosicrucian Order established its headquarters in San Jose in 1927. Reflecting its metaphysical and mystic background, the compound featured Egyptian-influenced buildings and grounds.

Predating the Rosicrucians' endeavors was an "Egyptomania" phenomenon that occurred in the early 1920s. Particularly infectious in Southern California, where a comparable Mediterranean climate no doubt encouraged entrepreneurs to adopt it, the Egyptian Revival was brought on in part by the discovery of King Tutankhamen's tomb in 1922. An impromptu and short-lived Egyptian-inspired building boom reinforced the concept of anything goes in California. For several years, hotels, apartments, movie theaters, car repair garages, real estate offices, plunges, and cafes received the Egyptian touch.

The heyday of California's programmatic past coincided with two developments, one local, one national. The rise of filmmaking in Hollywood and the widespread acceptance of the affordable automobile would combine to make California, and particularly Southern California, a hotbed of unusual architecture in the 1920s and 1930s.

Top. Motion picture art director Harry Oliver's 1921 design for the Irvin Willat Studio on Washington Boulevard in Culver City provided a direct link from Hollywood to the roadside. *Above*. The portable windmill stores of Van de Kamp's bakery are constructed in assembly-line fashion, ca 1921. *Opposite*. An early Van de Kamp's retail outlet designed by Harry Oliver.

The influence of Hollywood on California's programmatic tradition was very direct. The tone of fantasy was encouraged once the studios congregated in and around Hollywood, with the architecture and sets associated with movie making affecting the local environment. While most early studio architecture remained nondescript, several studios did create facades that matched the fantasy of the filming behind their gates. Around 1910, the Selig Studio in Edendale, a few miles northeast of downtown Los Angeles, was constructed to look like nearby San Gabriel Mission, complete with tower and bells. By 1921, Charlie Chaplin and his brother Sid had completed their studio at Sunset and La Brea in a series of buildings in the English Tudor Style. Out in Culver City, Thomas Ince built his Ince Studio Building (1919) in a graceful adaptation of a Southern mansion.

Several blocks away, studio head Irvin Willat went one step further in bringing Hollywood onto the streets when he employed set designer Harry Oliver to construct a studio headquarters for him in 1921 on highly traveled Washington Boulevard. In a head-spinning evocation of a fairy-tale witch's house straight out of Hansel and Gretel, Oliver transferred his cinematic set skills to the public sector. With this building, the connection between fantasy and reality was firmly made. The studio building remained as a local landmark until 1929, when it was purchased by producer Ward Lascelle and moved to Beverly Hills where it became his residence.

After designing the Willat Studio, Harry Oliver, who was also an art director for Fox and Metro Stu-

Top. **Another Harry Oliver design, the whimsical Tam o' Shanter Inn (1922) on Tropico Boulevard near Griffith Park was a popular eatery for the movie crowd from nearby studios and also inaugurated the region's first car service.**
Crossover. **A dramatic intrusion into suburbia, the set for Douglas Fairbanks' film *Robin Hood*, Santa Monica Boulevard near La Brea Avenue, 1922.**

dios, continued to use his movie background in various building projects outside the studio confines. Using a collection of postcards for inspiration, he created English thatched-roof apartments and Egyptian-inspired flats. Having caught the public's eye, he was soon asked to design the Van de Kamp's Bakery retail outlets for Lawrence Frank and Theodore Van de Kamp in 1921. On his clients' request, Oliver built the bakery outlets in the shape of small-scale Dutch windmills. As with the Willat Studio, the architect dramatized their appearance to make them more eye-catching. They were also to be portable so that in the event a location wasn't profitable they could be easily loaded on a truck and moved. Placed throughout Southern California, the dozens of fanciful structures again made a direct connection from studio

lot to the urban roadside that further fueled California's car-bound reputation.

Pleased with their bakery design, the Van de Kamp family employed Oliver for another venture on the "outskirts" of Los Angeles near Glendale. Montgomery's Country Inn, which would later be named the Tam o' Shanter, opened in 1922 on Tropico Avenue, later renamed Los Feliz Boulevard. Again following the family's wishes, Oliver designed a structure that would attract the interest of people driving by: "Make it fanciful. Make it a real standout. I want it to look like something out of Normandy," was owner Lawrence Frank's request. Oliver complied by creating another structure that looked like a transplanted movie set. Using a visual language similar to the one he used for the Willat Studio, Oliver created the roadside

Top. **The remains of D. W. Griffith's *Intolerance* set provided a photo-op for tourists near the intersection of Hollywood and Sunset Boulevards, ca 1917.** *Middle.* **Hollywood sets compound the intrusion of fantasy into the reality of everyday life, ca 1920.** *Bottom.* **Little Mary's Realty at 6002 Hollywood Boulevard adds a theatrical touch to Hollywood Boulevard, ca 1918.**

stop as a rambling fairy-tale structure complete with wavy rooflines, lopsided windows, and handmade lanterns partially trimmed in neon. The interior featured aged walls and soft curves that resembled the cottage of Snow White. The restaurant also initiated car service, thereby making it the first in California to do so.

Compounding the fantasy aspect of Los Angeles and reinforcing the Hollywood connection, the buildings gave visitors and Angelenos glimpses of the illusion being created behind the studio walls as they drove around the city. The set for D. W. Griffith's *Intolerance* was built in 1916 at the corner of Sunset and Hollywood Boulevards. It displayed a

Above. Hollywoodland, with "Wolf's Lair" in the foreground, was a real estate development which began in 1923, infusing the movie capital with additional fantasy imagery. *Below*. The Egyptian Theater, home of the first movie premiere, offered movie fantasy at 6712 Hollywood Boulevard. Architect: Meyer and Holler, 1922. *Opposite page: Top*. The roadside in an urban context. The Zulu Hut on Ventura Boulevard, "half a mile beyond Universal Studios," ca. 1928. Owner: Raymond McKee. *Middle*. The Wigwam, "the most beautiful fruit furniture and basket store in America," Foothill Boulevard, Arcadia, ca 1926. *Bottom*. The Barrel Inn, 1525 North San Fernando Road, Glendale, ca 1927.

RAMOND McKEE
"ZULU CHIEF"

The home of the famous "Wigwam Orange Ju...
Foothill Boulevard   Arcadia Californi...
Seven miles East of Pasadena.
Phone Arcadia 101 W.

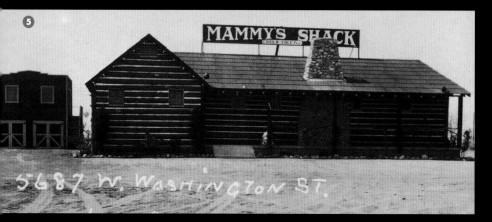

trussed and false-fronted Babylonia that was viewed by local residents and tourists years after the movie was filmed. Near the intersection of Santa Monica Boulevard and La Brea Avenue, the massive castle for Douglas Fairbanks' 1922 film *Robin Hood* towered surrealistically over the neighborhood. Several years later at the same location, the city of Baghdad would be created for another Fairbanks swashbuckler in an even larger set that was visible for blocks surrounding the studio. Throughout the area, false skies painted on billboard-size backdrops could be seen along the streets, while wooden dinosaur skeletons bordered studio fences. "Hollywood" appeared to be everywhere.

The influence of the movie studios on local architecture was noted early on by the media in several articles dating from the late 1920s. A 1928 article in the *Ice Cream Trade Journal* wrote in response to the highly profitable roadside stands:

"If this manufacturer had traveled through California without pre-warning and without stopping to investigate, he might have come away with the idea that the movie people had been so rash as to invade even the residential districts of the cities there in establishing 'locations.' What else could a tourist think who, knowing by hearsay something of the prevalence of studios and the studio folk in

Washington Boulevard in Culver City was one of Southern California's first urban entertainment strips. Jammed with Prohibition-era roadhouses, cafes, bars, dance halls, movie studios, and roadside attractions with programmatic overtones, it was a popular tourist and local attraction. Starting at the eastern city limits near Fairfax Avenue: (1) The entrance to Mission Village, 5675 Washington Boulevard, a tourist camp and Indian museum, ca 1929. (2) Teepee motel rooms at Mission Village. (3) Investors' brochure for the original Mission Village concept, 1928. (4) Monkey Farm, Fairfax and Washington, ca 1925. (5) Mammy's Shack, 5687 Washington Boulevard, ca 1930. (6) King's Tropical Inn menu. (7) King's Tropical Inn, 5741 Washington Boulevard, ca 1926. (8) King's Tropical Inn, ca 1933. (9) The Big Fireplace, ca 1927. (10) Jerry's Cabin Cafe, ca 1926. (11) The Hoosegow, 7732 Washington Boulevard, ca 1929. (12) Jesse James Cabin, 11950 Washington Boulevard, ca 1927.

that state, found himself whirling past gigantic ice cream freezers, snow block Eskimo igloos glowing in an electric aurora borealis by night, mammoth ice cream cones, and sparkling ice caverns, all established on the city streets or at vantage points along the open highway?"

The contribution of art director to the architectural landscape of Los Angeles was noted in the January 1926 issue of *The Motion Picture Director* magazine: "In California, I believe, before elsewhere in America, a direct influence of the cinema upon the House that Jack Builds becomes evident. Here may be traced even the story types. A popular story is made having as locale a mythical village in middle Europe. And appear as if by magic, in the way of the West, castles and cottages patterned after castles and cottages of that village, existing only yesterday as a vision of the art director, today in wallboard and plaster on the studio lot, and tomorrow as ashes in an incinerator, where the studio refuse is destroyed. Stories of ancient Egypt appear—an entire block becomes reminiscent of Karnac and Luxor, sheltering countless dreamy-

Above. **The Ham Tree, 8641 Washington Boulevard, ca 1927.** *Left.* **The Green Mill, Washington and National Boulevards, ca. 1923.**

Right. Ince Studios, 9336 Washington Boulevard, 1921.
Below. Fatty Arbuckle's Plantation Club, 10950 Washington Boulevard, 1926.

eyed and full-lipped Cleopatras from as far away as Far Rockaway even, who may lead you to a vacant seat. China and Russia have been seen in a photoplay. Then again on a street in 'Our Town.'"

When it opened on October 18, 1922, the Egyptian Theater on Hollywood Boulevard was a movie palace on a par with the ancient tomb of Tutankhamen, which would be discovered a month later. Lured to Hollywood by real estate developer Charles Toberman, Sid Grauman brought a touch of the Nile to the middle of filmland. A magnificent blending of kitsch and class, the structure was designed by the firm of Meyer and Holler. The forecourt featured palm trees, hieroglyphics, and stores masquerading as a bazaar. Above the main entrance an actor costumed as an Egyptian guard roamed the parapet

Top left. The Kone Inn, 402 York Boulevard, Eagle Rock, ca 1931. *Top right.* The Igloo. 4302 West Pico Boulevard, ca 1928. *Bottom left.* The Ice Palace, 3400 Crenshaw Boulevard, ca 1929. *Bottom right.* The Freezer, 3641 4th Avenue, Los Angeles, ca 1932. *Opposite.* The Big Cone, various locations throughout Southern California, ca 1928.

announcing the start of each performance. Attendants attired in period outfits led patrons to their seats. Here Sid Grauman initiated and refined the movie premiere by drawing movie stars and the attention of the world to his Hollywood theater. It was another grand illusion on the city streets.

While this concentration of movie-town architecture became synonymous with Hollywood, the rest of Southern California was beginning to blossom with unusual architecture. By the mid-1920s, California's programmatic tradition had begun in earnest. A bright economy, rampant speculation and inexpensive real estate, endless boosterism, the geographic layout of the region, and the acceptance and fostering of the car culture all combined to make an environment conducive to this building type.

Top. Robert Stacy-Judd's Aztec Hotel, 311 West Foothill Boulevard, Monrovia, 1925. *Above*. Rendering of Robert Stacy-Judd's Soboba Hot Springs resort, 1924. *Opposite page:* (1) Aztec Hotel facade. (2) Lobby of the Aztec Hotel. (3) Restaurant and soda fountain of the Aztec Hotel. (4) Several of the Native American–inspired bungalows at Soboba Hot Springs resort, ca 1925.

Proliferating in a short span of time, entrepreneurship, imagination, and the ingenuity of the small business person all contributed heavily to the success of many of these retail buildings. Promoted by the media as typical of Southern California, the buildings supposedly lined the streets, but this notion was somewhat off base. The wide distances separating various suburban communities contradicted that image. The buildings were more like exclamation points along the highway. Still, there were far more of these structures in the Los Angeles area than was generally thought, and when added together they set California apart from every other region.

Fortune magazine, in a story about the lucrative American roadside, reinforced this idea of "the land of the bizarre" in a caption accompanying the photo of a stand featuring an oversized ice cream carton:

"The eye is quicker than the brain and therefore Freda Farms near Hartford, Connecticut does very nicely. So do stands built like tamales, tea rooms built like tea pots, papier-mache owls lettered 'I Scream,' laughing swine with Neon teeth (again a tamale stand), and in fact almost any eye-widening outlandishness you can imagine. To behold such haywire crowned and seated in its ultimate glory, you must go to California."

Throughout California, the main roads leading into metropolitan areas were the obvious place for refreshment stands, eateries, and other businesses to solicit the auto trade with unusual imagery. Enticing motorists who were driving by at thirty-five miles per hour required eye-catching and flashy solutions. While many commercial ventures warranted locations that would provide a financial return in relation to their investment, these simple roadside businesses could afford to be placed in less desirable and out-of-the-way locations. Hence many of these roadside vernacular buildings could be found scattered in both more out-of-the-way urban and rural settings. The only mandate was that they be situated near or on a highly traveled street or thoroughfare.

Crossover and *Far right*. **Tugboat and lighthouse residence of a Hollywood starlet along Pacific Coast Highway, Trancas Beach, ca 1932.** *Right.* **A roadside refreshment stand and tea room, Malibu, ca 1929.**

In Duarte, on Foothill Boulevard, the Indian Village and Zanzibar Cafe (ca 1926) was typical of these roadside stops. The combination roadside stand and restaurant catered to the traveler and tourist heading into Los Angeles by selling produce and orange juice. Clearly not Native American in image, the Indian Village was exotic looking and enticed customers to stop in. Later named the Wigwam, it featured food and furniture made from local orange wood. Closer to town, but in an area still considered rural in the 1920s, the Zulu Hut (ca 1926) on Ventura Boulevard near Universal Studios was a cafe that attempted a similar exotic reference: Africa. Owner Raymond McKee dressed his servers in grass skirts and blackface for an "authentic" trip to the "Dark Continent." Several three-dimensional oranges and lemons could be found in the regions outside L.A. where "fresh-squeezed orange juice" was available almost everywhere, especially at the Mount Baldy Inn (1927), a stucco re-creation of the mountain range it faced.

Within L.A.'s urban spread, the evolving commercial strip of Washington Boulevard in Culver City

Above. **Tiree Castle, an eighteen-room residence built by Alexander Maclean in Alhambra, California, ca 1916.** *Opposite page: Top.* **Moorish-influenced bungalow apartments, 1042 South Ardmore, Los Angeles, ca 1928.** *Middle left.* **A common sight throughout 1920s Los Angeles, fairy-tale houses, 6450 Maryland Drive, ca 1929.** *Middle right.* **An Ocean Park residence conjures visions of Saracenic royalty, ca 1915.** *Bottom.* **Rich Middle Eastern detailing adorns a Pasadena residence, ca 1926.**

was littered with a series of fantasy buildings. A precursor to filmland's famed Sunset Strip, this main artery to the beach also served as a direct route to the many studios in Culver City. Washington Boulevard's popularity was enhanced during Prohibition by its reputation as a stretch of roadway on which one could score some illegal booze, gamble, and "raise a little Cain." This series of buildings, all with programmatic intonations, lined the street from the eastern border of Culver City westward. Among them were the following: the Mission Village (1929), the Monkey Farm (1925), the Fireplace (1927), Mammy's Shack (1930), King's Tropical Inn (1926), Lighthouse Gardens (1927), the Royal Barbecue (1924), Jerry's Cabin Cafe (1926), The Hoosegow (1927), the Ham Tree (1929), Jesse James Cabin (1928), the Green Mill (1919), the Irvin Willat Studio (1921), Thomas Ince Studio (1919), the Barrel Cafe (1934), Fatty Arbuckle's Plantation Club (1926), and the Pup Cafe (1930), among others. In describing the Royal Barbecue, a 1924 trade magazine gave uncanny insight to the place and time of this rural/urban roadside stop:

"The quaintness of a medieval inn, as idealized and enhanced by the spirit of jazz, is the atmosphere that has been achieved by the little Royal Barbecue Inn which has risen on Washington Boulevard between Los Angeles and the beach. The building was designed by its owner and manager, Mrs. Josephine Lanzit, in co-operation with her brother, E. J. Reutler, who was also the builder. It is one of those rambling crazily artistic structures, imitating a tumble-down medieval dwelling, but for all its playful imitation of age, not only modern but distinctively futuristic in effect and charming, like a very young girl masquerading in her own idea of an ancient costume. There is probably no stretch of highway on the Pacific coast which is more constantly traveled by pleasuring auto parties than that

Opposite page: Top. **Samson's Tire Works, later U.S. Tires, was a re-creation of an Assryian palace at 5675 Telegraph Road in the City of Commerce. Architect: Morgan Wells and Clements, 1929.** *Bottom.* **Calmos #1 Service Station, 4982 Hollywood Boulevard, 1923.** *Above.* **Persian Market, 12137 Washington Place, Los Angeles. Architect: George M. Thomas, 1929.**

between the beach and Los Angeles, and so those who serve the pleasure-seeking public have not been slow in congregating on it. A number of the largest and most brilliant road-house cafes like the Green Mill and Plantation are located there and also a large number of 'barbecued sandwich' shacks line the road."

In time the urban strip became the most viable location for the ever-increasing number oddball buildings. Some of the most popular imagery on the byways during this time was reserved for businesses selling ice cream products. Alluding to colder climes were ice cream stands such as the Igloo (1928), complete with miniature polar bear and frozen ghost frigate bathed in the Northern Lights, the Ice Palace (1929), and the Ice Castle (1928).

The Big Cone (1928) was a chain of ice cream stands in the shape of a twenty-foot sugar cone made of metal and placed from Laguna Beach to the San Fernando Valley. The Big Freezer (1927) chain was owned by United Sweet Shops of Glendale, California. Numbering twenty by 1929, their appeal to the automobile was no mistake. The old-fashioned freezer, originally painted an authentic wood brown, was later repainted white with red hoops to be visible from a long distance. Company owners claimed the following as one of the many advantages of the Big Freezer:

"The building advertises its own product and is considered by authorities to be the most successful wayside store so far invented. The traveler can not mistake the purpose of the freezer when he sees it

Opposite page: *Top left.* Angelus Abbey, 1500 Compton Boulevard, Compton, effectively used biblical imagery in selling cemetery plots, ca 1928. *Top right.* Evangelist Aimee Semple McPherson created a mansion in Elsinore worthy of Ali Baba, ca 1930. *Bottom.* The Black Tent, a roadside stand on South Palm Canyon Drive in Palm Springs, 1937. *This page: Top left.* A real estate office on Ventura Boulevard near Van Nuys, ca 1928. *Top right.* Real estate offices for the Girard subdivision, Ventura and Topanga Canyon Boulevards, San Fernando Valley, 1928. *Middle.* The Calpet Super Service Station, 3237 Wilshire Boulevard. Architect: Roland E. Coate, 1928. *Bottom.* Appropriately attired female attendants pose on opening day. Note ornate cashier's booth and waiting room in background.

Grauman's Chinese Theatre, 6925 Hollywood Boulevard.
Architect: Meyer and Holler, 1927.

ahead of him beside of the highway. He knows that there is a place where ice cream is sold. The plan of having a building cry its own product is of distinct advantage in wayside places because if the automobile driver does not sense the fact that a certain store along the way sells ice cream until he is past it, then that possible customer is lost for he can not, in the face of traffic, turn around and come back."

To further attract roadside attention, Big Freezer owners installed a revolving handle that they claimed increased sales by 50 percent the first week it was available. The simple building made of steel had no plumbing, tables, or toilets (employees were encouraged to use neighboring businesses for their needs), but just a simple counter where prepackaged bulk ice cream was sold because "the ice cream for the most part is eaten in automobiles." This pared-down layout allowed for the buildings to be moved at will if the location proved unsatisfactory or if the lot was slated for a permanent building. Perfectly dovetailing with California's expanding urban car culture, the Big Freezers were not located in the open country as many other wayside stands were, but placed "in cities on vacant lots in sections where traffic is considerable but always where there is ample parking space for a car to stop in front."

As the Southern California geography began to fill in through rapid development, many of these way-side places found themselves in transitional locations between open country and suburban towns. Characteristic of this change was the Aztec Hotel (1925). Located on Foothill Boulevard, which was a major highway leading into Los Angeles, the Aztec Hotel was built in the suburban community of Monrovia. Designed by architect Robert Stacy-Judd from his offices in Hollywood, it was described in a trade magazine of the period as being "designed after Aztec and Mayan styles with furnishings and fixtures carried out in weird and fascinating details which leave little to the

This page: Top. **The Mandarin Market, 1248 Vine Street. Architect: M. L. Gregory, 1928.** *Above.* **Airplane Cafe, Ventura Boulevard, San Fernando Valley, ca 1927.** *Opposite.* **An observation tower serves as a real estate gimmick allowing potential property owners to peruse their lot. Beverly Glen and Wilshire Boulevards, ca 1922.**

imagination." Stacy-Judd focused a major part of his career on re-creating the architecture of ancient North American cultures. Before this commission he had toyed with various other exotic period-revival buildings including a proposal for an Egyptian-inspired theater in nearby Arcadia. Although his later influences were distinctly Mayan, he felt Mayan architecture wasn't as widely known. The hotel was named "the Aztec" because he speculated it was a name more familiar to the general public. Stacy-Judd meticulously researched many of the details for the hotel before modifying and adapting them to a modern California setting. Included in the hotel design were stylized Mayan interiors for the lobby that expressed the feel of entering a temple dwelling. In an odd juxtaposition, an adjoining coffee shop and soda fountain also received the Mayan treatment.

Further exercising his creative muscle, Stacy-Judd was engaged to create an Indian village–style resort at Soboba Hot Springs some ninety miles east of Los Angeles near San Jacinto. Between 1924 and 1927, a series of cottages were interspersed on the hillside representing various Native American settlements. Taking stylistic liberties, his freestanding rooms were playful interpretations of Pueblo, Hopi, Yuma, and other Southwest tribal dwellings. A proposed hotel and bathhouse in similar styles never materialized, but the dozen cottages built were extremely popular with visitors at the time. Another resort closer to Los Angeles in the Chatsworth area was also to be a cluster of Mayan and Indian structures in a development called Twin Lakes Park. Advertised in 1927 as the

Below. **The Tower Auto Court, 11580 Ventura Boulevard, Studio City, ca 1932.** *Opposite page: Top.* **The Allessandro, "An Adobe Hotel In The Romantic Ramona Country," Hemet, ca 1938.** *Middle.* **Cabot's Old Indian Pueblo, Desert Hot Springs, ca 1941.** *Bottom.* **Kenyon's Desert Plunge, El Centro, 1929.**

Top. Cliff Dwellers Cafe, 3591 Beverly Boulevard, Los Angeles, ca 1925. Owner: Cort Fox. *Above.* The Mountains, Garfield Boulevard at Whittier Boulevard, Montebello, 1928. *Opposite.* TeePee Barbecue, 5231 E. Second Street, Belmont Shores, Long Beach, ca 1930.

"Homesite of the Maya Village," the resort had an entry gate in a vaguely Mayan style, but again, a proposed clubhouse and cabins never materialized.

Robert Stacy-Judd created several other buildings and residences in modified Mayan and Pueblo styles. Cliff-dwelling-style apartments in Elysian Park, a church in Ventura, a Masonic temple, and several homes in North Hollywood were built in the twenties and thirties. Still, most of his more ostentatious commissions were never realized.

The idea of Los Angeles as an exotic destination was long promoted by the region's real estate agents and promoters and supported in many of the buildings that were built there in the twenties. Many of the buildings transcended the mere convention of reviving historical styles. For example, the proximity of California's desert inspired a wide selection of Moorish and Mediterranean buildings that were spread throughout Southern California. Angelus Abbey, a cemetery complex in Compton,

flaunted palm trees, tiled domes, and Moroccan-style arches. In the Mar Vista district, a drive-in open-air market of Middle Eastern design was built with a dome-topped tower and a colonnade of Oriental arches. The real estate offices for the Girard subdivision (1928) at Topanga Canyon and Ventura Boulevards were fashioned in a similar mosque-and-minaret motif, but their interiors were vacant, thus the buildings serving as props. In 1927, Calpet Petroleum built an extravagant station catering to wealthy Angelenos on Wilshire Boulevard. Located in what was then one of L.A.'s most fashionable shopping districts, the station had a vaguely Middle Eastern tone. A Tunisian color scheme of red, tan, and black was used for the tile work. Catering to its 55 percent female customers were a "colored liveried footman" and a team of eight service men outfitted in maroon jackets, white shirts, black bow ties, breeches, and puttees. The ladies' room was outfitted with Venetian mirrors and a "red leather topped wicker settee with lovely pillows, a number of rockers, a taupe rug, and smoking stands." The

Top. Promotional car for the Pumpkin Inn. *Left.* Interior of the Pumpkin Palace, ca 1930. *Crossover.* The Pumpkin Palace, 3611 Magnolia Boulevard, Burbank, 1927. *Opposite.* Its days as a cafe/roadhouse complete, the Pumpkin Palace receives an innovative re-use as the Valley Gospel Center, ca 1935.

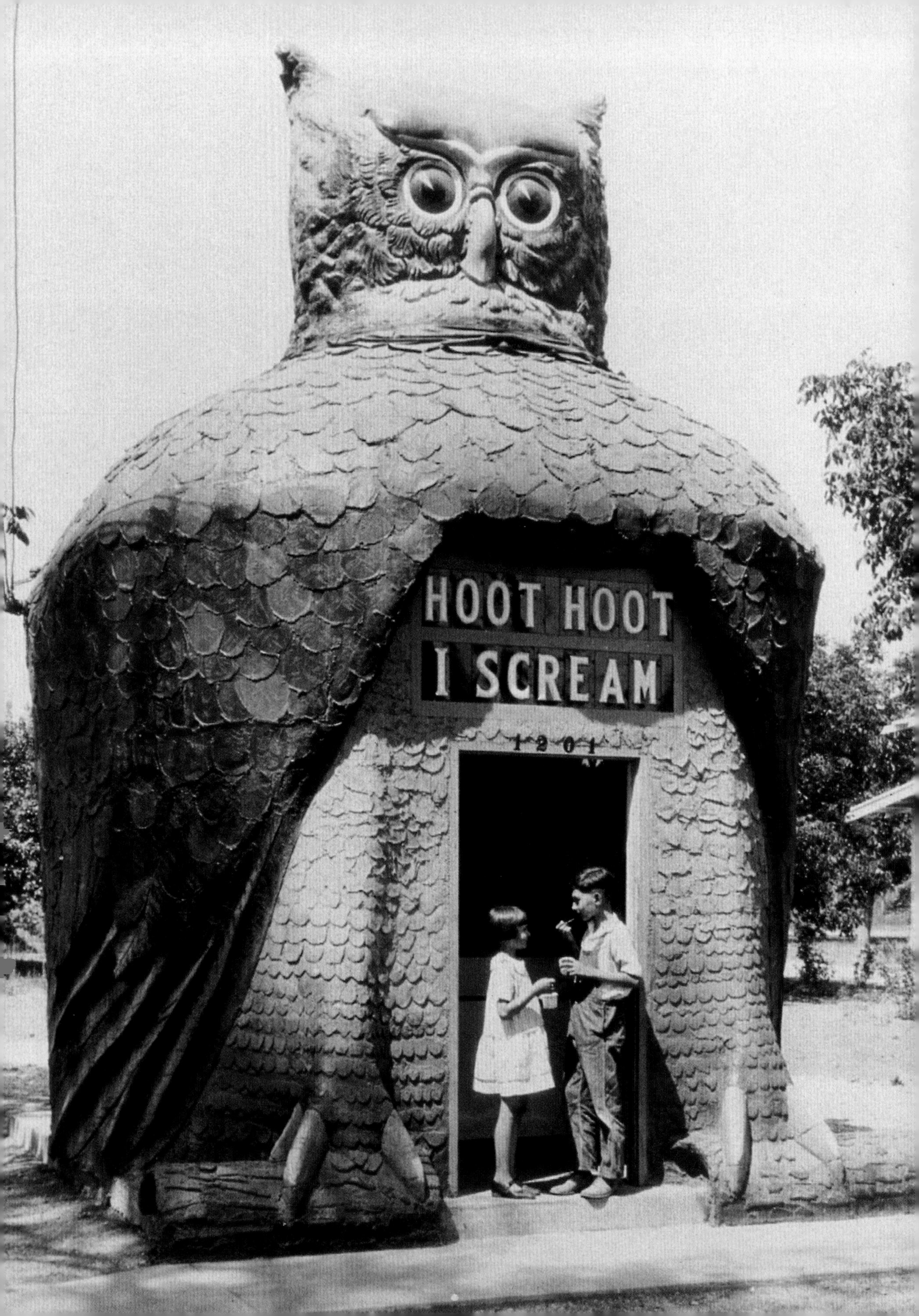
HOOT HOOT
I SCREAM
1201

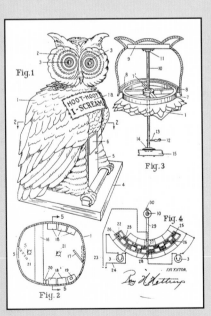

Opposite. Hoot Hoot I Scream. Original location Valley Boulevard, San Gabriel Valley. Moved to 8711 Long Beach Boulevard, South Gate, ca 1930. Owner: Tilly Hattrup. *Top.* The Pig Cafe, 400 block of La Brea Avenue at Rosewood Avenue, Hollywood, ca 1934. *Above.* Patent drawings for the Hoot Hoot I Scream stand showing the mechanism for rotating the head and blinking the Cadillac headlight eyes.

Opposite page: Top. The Bulldog Cafe, 1153 West Washington Boulevard, Los Angeles, 1928. *Bottom*: Sphinx Realty Company, 537 North Fairfax Avenue, Los Angeles, 1926. *This page: Top*. The Toed Inn at its original location, 12008 Channel Road, Santa Monica Canyon, Santa Monica, 1931. *Middle*. Toed Inn menu. *Bottom*. After a devastating flood in 1938 that flushed the original Toed towards the ocean, it was rebuilt on higher ground at 12008 Wilshire Boulevard in West Los Angeles.

main room was enclosed by wrought iron gates and a white cash register rested on a marble-topped table beneath a chandelier. Samson's Tire Works (1929), on the outskirts of Los Angeles, paid tribute to the connection of oil and the Middle East with its magnificent re-creation of an Assyrian palace. Designed by the firm of Morgan, Walls, and Clements, the main building and wall fronted the street while behind the decorative walls a modern factory churned out tires with no pretensions to fantasy.

Grauman's Chinese Theatre (1927) contributed a grand pastiche of Asian elements suggesting a mysterious and exotic location. Perfectly matching the illusion of moviemaking, the theater borrowed pieces of Chinese architecture and put them together facing the main street of the movies, Hollywood Boulevard. Acknowledging the importance of the automobile, an open forecourt gestured directly to the street and became the

central plaza for the theater's famed premieres. An extravagant interior was lavishly appointed with murals, chandeliers, and intricate details such as the costumes of the ushers and the faucets in the washrooms. Along the same Asian lines, the Mandarin Market (1929), a drive-in arcade on Vine Street, was the commercial equivalent to the high-toned Chinese Theatre. An incongruous Chilitown Cafe, which anchored one of the retail outlets, spoke much about the seriousness of programmatic imagery.

Above. **The Round House, 250 North Virgil Avenue, Los Angeles, 1927. Near the intersection where the Round House was located, at Virgil and Beverly, could be found the best concentration of programmatic buildings in Los Angeles: The Cliff Dwellers, a Chili Bowl, the Freezer, a Van de Kamp's windmill, and Barkies.** *Opposite.* **The Mushrooms, 3500 W. Olive Avenue, ca 1928.**

In extending the search for more exotic solutions, Native American imagery was tapped not only for its references to the old West but also for the intrigue of relatively obscure ancient American civilizations. Satisfying this criterion was the Mayan Theater (1927) in downtown Los Angeles, the Cliff Dwellers Cafe (1927) on Beverly Boulevard, the TeePee drive-in restaurant (1931) in the Belmont Shores district of Long Beach, the Hotel Tahquitz (1929) in Palm Springs, the pueblo-inspired Alessandro Hotel in Hemet (1928), the Tower Auto Court (1929) on Ventura Boulevard, and the Mission Village (1932) near Culver City, which offered a range of Native American styles in a motel, trailer court, and tourist complex.

The golden age of the programmatic lasted for approximately ten years, from 1924 through 1934. Within that span the best buildings in this architectural category were built: the Hoot Hoot I Scream stand (1930), the Pup and Bulldog Cafes (c. 1930 and 1927, respectively), the Sphinx Realty building (1926), the Mushrooms restaurant (c. 1928), the Zep Diner (1930), the Hollywood Flower Pot (c. 1930), the Cream Can (c. 1928), the Tamale (1928), the Toed Inn (1931), the Pumpkin Palace (c. 1927), the Mother Goose Pantry (1929), the Big Red Piano (1930), and many others. And most had stories to tell.

The Brown Derby (1926) symbolized the apex of this building spree. One of the most popular of the programmatic buildings, it owed much of its fame to its celebrity pedigree. The owners included film producer and taste arbiter Herbert Somborn, once married to Gloria Swanson; Broadway wit Wilson Mizner, who is credited with naming it; Charles "Buddy" Rogers; Jack Warner; and the department store scions Tom and Wilbur May. All were interested in investing in a place that stayed open late and offered good, substantial food. Somborn reasoned that "a place that served fine American dishes made with the freshest and best raw materials obtainable, prepared with skill and experience a

Chili Bowl owner Arthur Whizin was the consummate programmatic entrepreneur. Starting in 1931 Whizin managed to open several Chili Bowls a year, completing twenty-three within a decade. His popular cafes had a loyal following and to further promote them he sponsored a baseball team, raffled rides on the Chili Bowl airplane, and advertised his restaurants on a speedboat which crossed the Catalina Channel laden with Fanchon and Marco showgirls. World War II ended Whizin's reign with the exception of the Pico Boulevard outlet, which was kept open to accommodate nearby workers at the Santa Monica Douglas aircraft plant. After the war many of the Chili Bowls became Punch and Judy ice cream parlors, but they too disappeared by the end of the 1940s. *Top.* A freshly built Chili Bowl gets the finishing touch, a 1933. *Crossover.* The original Chili Bowl at 3012 Crenshaw Boulevard. Opening day April 4, 1931. *Opposite page: Left.*

place so distinctive in architecture that, once seen or heard about, it would never again be forgotten." Opening night guests included Mary Pickford, Sid Grauman, Loretta Young, Bebe Daniels, and Corinne Griffith. Far from being a gourmand's paradise, the Brown Derby initially offered hot dogs, hamburgers, grilled cheese sandwiches, chili, tamales, coffee, tea, milk, and near beer—in other words, diner fare. Being across the street from the famed Ambassador Hotel and Cocoanut Grove secured a steady clientele of stars that in turn brought the fans, which made the Derby an instant and ongoing hit.

Joining the evolving carscape was a host of advertising sculptures posted along the streets that added another dimension to the byways. Reviled by critics as another element of blight to an overcrowded streetscape, these three-dimensional figures on pedestals were used to sell just about any product a local resident might consume or any place a local resident might visit. Using the same eye-catching principle as programmatic buildings, the sculptures were meant to grab your attention for a billboard moment and fade away just as quickly. The Richfield gas station featured a model of driver Barney Oldfield and his race car. A Colonial Style dame surmounted the Carthay Circle Theater pedestal (1927); bathing beauties frol-

The Rabbit, a retail rabbit farm on South Figueroa Street, ca 1935.

icked on the Sea Breeze Beach Club sign, and Ye Bull Pen Inn had a majestic bull atop its platform. Another curious element to the streetscape was the miniature golf courses, which sprouted up almost overnight in a craze that started in 1930. Bringing a whole new level of zaniness to the Los Angeles area, this transitory fad took advantage of a relatively low investment and the large supply of vacant lots. Hundreds of these courses were found throughout the city, and miniature cabins, rock grottoes, windmills, and rustic bridges were added to city corners everywhere. One ambitious course took the theme of the frozen North and constructed an oversized igloo, abandoned ghosts ships, and snowbound paths. Movie star Mary Pickford invested in one grandiose course at the corner of Wilshire and La Cienega Boulevards in Beverly Hills in 1930. The Wilshire Links course featured a Zig Zag Moderne advertising pylon that housed a corner office and refreshment stand. Scattered throughout the layout were stylized palm trees that looked like props from a German Expressionist film.

The Depression, during which many of these structures were built, rarely deterred the construction of programmatic buildings. The inexpensive nature of a modest building and the still-affordable land made many of these investments worthwhile.

Texaco Airplane, 12000 Ventura Boulevard at Ventura Place, Studio City, ca 1940.

Some of these ventures proved so successful that the owners went on to construct multiple units and even chains. The Twin Barrels drive-in (1928) and the Bucket (ca. 1935) were among those that built several units. The Sanders System drive-in restaurants, in the shape of giant coffee pots spouting steam, staked out major intersections and opened three units in July 1930. In Tinseltown tradition, klieg lights crossed the skies, bands were broadcast live, and celebrities were on hand to cut the ribbon. The Chili Bowl restaurants, with 23 units, outperformed most of its competitors. Started in 1931 by entrepreneur Arthur Whizin, their enormous success was due to the simple fare, affordable prices, and Whizin's tireless promotion. Found mostly in urban areas, the White Log Taverns, which originated in Oakland, spread forty units across California and into Oregon with the same "immaculate early American colonial style" log cabin. Out in the open, along California roads, the Jumbo Lemon Company produced their one-man booths from Yuma to Yreka along most of the main highways in California, and in small towns. The owners avoided large cities such as Los Angeles and San Francisco. The Giant Orange refreshment stands ran the length of the San Joaquin Valley on Highways 40, 50, and 99 with a total of sixteen stands at their peak.

The domination of programmatic structures in Southern California sometimes overshadowed the fact that these types of structures were actually

dispersed throughout the state. In addition to lemons and oranges, there were others. In San Jose the beacon from a forty-foot lighthouse that rose above the Grace Baptist Church could be seen for twenty miles in the Santa Clara Valley, so it was claimed. Merced had the Magnus Root Beer drive-in (ca 1934), an oversized root beer barrel. The first bona fide motel, the Motel Inn (1925), in San Luis Obispo, suggested an old mission with a replica of Santa Barbara's mission bell tower along Highway 101. In Carmel, the Tuck Box (1926), a tea shop, as well as other fairy-tale-like buildings, were built by local resident Hugh Comstock. The Bay Area sup-

plied numerous programmatic buildings on the highways leading into San Francisco. Windmill-shaped hotels and stands could be found in the East Bay and along El Camino Real and Bayshore Highway where restaurants such as Dinah's (ca 1925) addressed the road. The high density of San Francisco made it a difficult location to transpose the roadside sensibilities of programmatic

Above. **The Zep Diner, 515 W. Florence Avenue, Los Angeles, ca 1928.** *Opposite page: Top.* **Mother Goose Pantry, 1959 East Colorado Boulevard, Pasadena, ca 1929.** *Bottom.* **Kids scramble over the giant shoe on opening day.**

architecture. Instead, period revival examples stood in for most mimetic architecture with theaters such as the Alhambra (1931) on Polk Street and the Alexandria (ca 1930) on Geary. In Berkeley, several commercial buildings and apartments including the Tupper and Reed Building (1927) appropriated the fantasy style of the late twenties and early thirties.

By the mid-1930s the programmatic building boom showed signs of exhaustion. While still lauded in the press, the programmatic style fell out of favor as new architectural styles began to appear. Los Angeles, always receptive to change, embraced the new Streamline Moderne Style, which was promoted by industrial designers and showcased in several national expositions. Almost instantly it became the style of choice for anything that was new, modern, and progressive. With the advent of clean lines and allusions to speed and the future, the construction of the old programmatic buildings began to dwindle. Only a few structures with programmatic leanings were able

to accommodate the style. Robert Derrah designed the Coca-Cola Company Building in 1936 in the industrial section of L.A. to look like a streamlined ocean liner. He also produced the Cross Roads of the World (1936) in Hollywood, an informal mall of assorted shops in various historical and period styles fitted around a stylized streamlined ship. Facing Sunset Boulevard at the end of the liner was a large pylon with a rotating globe trimmed in neon that beckoned autoists like a lighthouse. In San Francisco, the elegant Steinhart Aquarium (1939) also referenced the Streamline Moderne Style but in a way that suppressed a programmatic subtext. Back in L.A., the Streamline Diner (1935) on San Vincente successfully adopted the new styling in a tasteful restaurant, but it was the modern drive-in restaurant that supplanted the old

Above. **The Tamale, 6421 Whittier Boulevard, Montebello, ca 1928.** *Opposite page: Top.* **Parker-Judge Decorating Company, 224 Juanita Avenue, Los Angeles, ca 1930.** *Bottom.* **Ray L. Hommes Realty, 828 S. Robertson Boulevard, Los Angeles, ca 1932.**

Above. The Oil Can, Whittier Boulevard, East Los Angeles, ca 1933. *Left.* Barkies, 3649 Beverly Boulevard, Los Angeles, ca 1929. *Opposite.* The Cream Can, Los Angeles, 1928.

rules of the road. Here, gleaming buildings, especially those designed by Harry Werner and Wayne McAllister, grabbed customers off the street with their tall neon-lit pylons. Expressing everything that was modern, the drive-in restaurant became a preferred roadside model in the late 1930s.

The early 1940s were lean programmatic years as the specter of war effectively tightened construction. Once the war began, rationed building materials and travel limitations squelched an already moribund programmatic tradition. The war effort in Southern California did produce new methods and materials that would be used in the signage and statues, which in turn would become substitutes for many of the fast disappearing programmatic structures of the twenties. It was in this critical period of disfavor that some of the best programmatic build-

ings disappeared. Never intended for long-term use, the buildings' fragile nature made them vulnerable to adverse conditions, and a crowded wartime L.A. made demands on every parcel of premium land.

With Modernist principles fully embraced at the end of World War II, not much interest was concentrated on building new programmatic structures. Despite this postwar slump, L.A. saw several programmatic structures pop up: The Tail o' the Pup, opened by two ex-GIs in 1946, was featured in a *Life* magazine spread that showed premiere-type crowds clamoring for hot dogs. Drivers

Above. **The Orange Blossom, location unknown, ca 1927.**
Opposite. **The Jumbo Lemon, various locations throughout California, 1925.**

encountered a surrealistic vision on Olympic Boulevard, where a retail outlet dispensed stockings beneath a giant thirty-foot leg. The Sanderson Hosiery Company (1948), seizing on the advertising potential, inaugurated their company by hoisting movie celebrity Marie Wilson on a crane and releasing a giant garter from the gam. Up north, the Capitol Inn (1948) in Sacramento was built as a replica of what else—the state capitol.

Modernism crept into programmatic buildings in the slightest ways. Signs were the primary adjunct to pared-down retail outlets. In Currie's Ice Cream store (ca 1950), the giant cone formerly showcased atop the building was now discreetly placed near the sleek structure. As the old Van de Kamp's windmills disappeared from the street, modernizing included incorporating retail outlets into supermarkets or in some cases repackaging stores in modern buildings with only a neon sign as a

reminder of the three-dimensional building. Based on popular cartoon characters, the Beanie and Cecil drive-in restaurant (ca 1952) was housed in a pared-down box with a three-dimensional figure of Beanie, its sole programmatic reference.

Most of the programmatic statements of this era were reserved for signage, three-dimensional figures, and buildings that were simple to construct. This broadened idea of the programmatic shifted

Above. **The Sanders System drive-in restaurants, 7275 Beverly Boulevard, Los Angeles, 1931. Four Sanders restaurants debuted on July 3, 1930 with premiere-style festivities complete with klieg lights, Hollywood celebrities, and bands.** *Opposite page: Top.* **New owners of the Sanders giant coffee pot on Beverly Boulevard quickly dismantled the handle and spout and attached thousands of abalone shells to the exterior of the building complementing the seafood menu, 1938.** *Bottom.* **The interior of the Wilshire coffee pot.**

the emphasis of California's wacky reputation away from the old "dog and frog" standbys to these other areas. *Holiday* magazine noted this shift in a 1947 article entitled "California's Sunstruck Signs": "The bizarre competes with the screwloose in getting attention along the West Coast highways." Pictured was the Hangman's Tree (ca 1946), a San Fernando Valley eatery that advertised "warm beer and lousy food." Accompanying the sign was a mannequin hanging from a gallows.

The big figures and giant sculptures of men that were introduced in the fifties came courtesy of postwar technology. Their molded forms and generic interchangeable parts made them versatile

Opposite page: Top. **The Jail Cafe, 4212 Sunset Boulevard and 1207 W. Sixth Street, ca 1927.** *Bottom.* **Interior of the Jail Cafe featured jail cells and a jazz band.** *Below.* **The Hollywood Flower Pot, 1100 North Vine Street, Hollywood, ca 1933.**

advertising devices, and their low cost spread them statewide. In the Bay Area, the Doggie Diner (1948) snack shops had a variation on this theme in the giant cartoon dog's heads with chef hats that were hoisted on poles in front of each stand.

With an urban landscape rapidly closing in, the competition for customers' attention became acute and the luxury of open space and high visibility the first generation of buildings experienced was no longer there. The giant sign fulfilled the new roadside expectations. Russ Wendell realized this when he planned his Big Donut chain in 1949. By 1950 his dream was realized in the thirty-foot donut he erected at the corner of Century Boulevard and Normandie. In true Southern California fashion, he debuted his donut in December with the fanfare of a Hollywood premiere. Clowns, jugglers, and magicians performed, free coffee and donuts were handed out, and a trapeze artist swung from the middle of the donut hole. At

Christmastime, Santa and his reindeer were installed flying through the same hole. The store was an instant hit and Wendell went on to build ten more by 1956.

The California-born Googie Style, with its aggressive honesty, expressed materials, and sign presence, was a perfect segue from the more obvious revivalist architecture to a 1950s vocabulary. Expressing a "jet-age" mentality, this new style was suggestive of a programmatic ideal but avoided any figurative referencing. The hamburger stands and coffee shops that effectively used Googie imagery maintained the advertising qualities of a building as a sign but rarely committed to a three-dimensional object as a sign.

The tide of criticism directed at roadside buildings began to turn by the early sixties as popular tastes evolved. In an article entitled "Who Killed Our Monstrosities?" one author commented, "All the buildings look the same. Glass upon glass, tile upon tile, floor upon floor. Nothing distinctive, like that giant-shaped dog on Washington Boulevard that once was—of course—a hot dog house. Los Angeles could use a little more honesty like that." With the lapse of time, a clearer picture of

Above. **California Piano Supply Co., also known as the Big Red Piano, 2251 Venice Boulevard, Los Angeles, ca 1930.** *Opposite page: Top.* **Entrance to Mary Pickford's Wilshire Links miniature golf course, Wilshire Boulevard and La Cienega, 1930.** *Bottom.* **Mary Pickford's Wilshire Links.**

Bob's Airmail Service, 5453 Wilshire Boulevard, Los Angeles. Opened March 10, 1934 with a Hollywood premiere-style opening presided over by Wallace Beery.

the historical significance of these structures emerged and critics began to reassess the sensibilities of roadside architecture. Movements such as "Pop art" were also sympathetic to this architecture and were catalysts for removing the stigma associated with programmatic buildings in the twenties and thirties. But it was too late to save many of the structures as they crumbled or were dismantled to make way for new development.

While a few examples of the programmatic were built in the 1960s and 1970s, the shape of new buildings was confined to simpler forms. New building restrictions and sign ordinances precluded the more organic shapes of the past that wood and stucco allowed. Instead, the embellished box became a transitional form. The Showboat (1968), a restaurant chain, created the illusion of a Mississippi paddle wheeler by hanging the decorative boat elements on a basic box. Likewise, the Fleetwood Building (1987) on Ventura Boulevard in Woodland Hills fashioned a facade of Cadillac parts and painted the whole structure bright pink to draw more attention to the simple form. In Turlock, the United Equipment Company erected a building that looked like a two-story tractor for its

Opposite. **Twin Barrels, 7200 Beverly Boulevard, Los Angeles, ca 1932.** *This page: Top.* **Giant Barrel, Los Angeles, ca 1935.** *Middle.* **The Cookie Jar, location unknown, ca 1934.** *Bottom.* **A replica of Los Angeles City Hall, Sherman Oaks Service Station, 14583 Ventura Boulevard, Van Nuys, ca 1932.**

offices (1977). Again, to a simple box was added the apparatus of a bulldozer complete with a scraper pushing rocks. Visible from Highway 99, the building was based on one the owner had seen on a visit to Japan. The Shutter Shack (1977) in Westminster, California, exhibited the possibilities of a one-person box. Sheathed with some simple additions such as a lens and flash cube, the Shutter Shack was made to look like a 35 millimeter camera. While not the most satisfying of buildings, these structures did keep the programmatic style alive.

Just before the roadside tradition was entirely depleted in the 1980s, a renewal of the programmatic spirit ensued. Fueled in part by preservation

Opposite page: Top. **Boat apartments, Encinitas, ca 1928.** *Middle.* **Taube Plumbing Supply, location unknown, Los Angeles, ca 1927.** *Bottom.* **Noah's Ark, Highway 1, Leucadia, ca 1945.** *Above.* **The Toonerville Trolley, 1635 W. Manchester, Los Angeles, ca 1926.**

efforts and the wealth of information unearthed in reexamining the legacy of the roadside, new buildings were taking the place of those that were destroyed. The more successful examples bypassed a cloying nostalgia for a contemporary version of the programmatic past. The Hamburger That Ate L.A. (1989) was a three-dimensional facade of a hamburger accompanied by a stylized version of L.A. City Hall that had a bite extracted from it.

In the nineties, a certain legitimacy descended on architectural aberrations when established architects began to adopt a formalized version of roadside architecture. The Disney Company stepped up to the programmatic plate when they hired well-known architect Michael Graves to design a new Team Disney headquarters on their Burbank lot. A postmodern tour de force, the building features a pediment held up by massive statues of the "Seven Dwarfs." Across the street, a new animation building that is highly visible from

an adjacent freeway is rimmed by a stylized film-strip and capped with the alchemist's hat worn by Mickey Mouse in the "Sorcerer's Apprentice" sequence from the Disney film *Fantasia*. The hat is several stories high. Universal Studios also contributed to this themed architecture in its CityWalk (1991) expansion by Jon Jerde. A giant jukebox and an oversized surfboard were part of the fabricated, urban, street mall decorated with neon and other street elements. In Venice, California, the Chiat/Day advertising agency commissioned Frank Gehry to design their building (1992), which includes a giant pair of binoculars by Claes Oldenburg and Coosje van Bruggen. An immediate landmark, the binoculars serve as the portal to an underground parking structure. The stem of the binoculars contains several conference rooms lit by skylights that are fitted in the lenses.

As the new century begins, the outlook for a continuation of the roadside mentality is bright. Supported by revisionist theories, developments in Las Vegas, and an insatiable appetite for entertainment architecture, California and the rest of the country have already seen a flurry of activity. Giant french fries, Paul Bunyan–sized baseball caps, submarines extending out of shopping centers, and flying saucers slammed into electronic stores are but some of the manifestations of the programmatic reawakening. All the while, individuals, small firms, and well-known architects try to lure the consumer's eye by competing with one another in an overcrowded urban environment. Still tied to the rule of the road, the building's proliferation will certainly keep California crazy.

Opposite. **The Pyramid Cube University, Alhambra, ca 1932. Owner: Frank Ormsby.** *This page: Top.* **Garden of Eden Date Shop, Indio-Palm Springs Highway and Avenue 46, Indio, ca 1936. Owners: Mr. and Mrs. C. H. Eudemiller.** *Bottom left.* **The Giant Barrel, 5533 Huntington Drive (Route 66), Los Angeles, ca 1930.** *Bottom right.* **The Coffee Cup, 8901 Pico Boulevard, Los Angeles, ca 1935.**

This page: Top. Umbrella Service Station, General Petroleum Gas, 830 South La Brea, Los Angeles, 1930. *Middle.* The Dugout, 6157 Whittier Boulevard, Montebello, 1927. *Bottom.* The White Log Taverns, various locations throughout California, ca 1932. *Opposite page: Top.* The Brown Derby under construction, 1926. *Middle.* The Original Brown Derby, 3427 Wilshire Boulevard, Los Angeles, 1926. *Bottom.* To accommodate the large crowds, the Derby moved a half-block east in 1936, adding a large restaurant with patio.

Opposite page: Top. The Giant Orange, various locations along Highway 99, 1934. *Crossover.* The Motel Inn, Highway 101, San Luis Obispo, opened in December 1925. Architect and developer: Arthur Heineman. *Above.* 1930 Delta Crest Nursery and service station, Sacramento delta, ca 1929. *Right.* Grace Baptist Church, San Jose, ca 1925.

Top. The Tuck Box, Carmel, ca 1926. Architect: Hugh Comstock. *Above.* A tropical paradise in the center of downtown Los Angeles, Clifton's Cafeteria at 618 South Olive Street opened in 1931 in the depths of the Depression offering a "pay-what-you-wish" policy and free, nutritionally sound meals for those who could not afford to pay. Owner: Clifford Clinton. Architect: Welton Beckett. *Opposite.* Tupper and Reed Building, Berkeley, 1927. Architect: W. R. Yelland.

Opposite page: Top. The Garden of Allah, Savona Walk, Naples, Long Beach, ca 1930. Owner: Mrs. Vivian Laird. *Crossover.* Gay's Lion Farm, Valley Boulevard, El Monte, ca 1926. *Right.* Hawaiian Gardens, Artesia, ca 1926.

Opposite page: Top. The Coca-Cola Bottling Company, 1334 South Central Avenue, Los Angeles, 1936–37. Architect: Robert V. Derrah. *Bottom.* The Club Car, earlier known as Sardi's, 9543 Wilshire at San Vincente Boulevard, ca 1938. *Above.* Crossroads of the World, 6665 Sunset Boulevard, 1936–37. Architect: Robert V. Derrah. *Right.* Cross Roads of the World, interior court.

Above. The Darkroom, 5730 Wilshire Boulevard, Los Angeles, 1938. *Opposite page: Top*. Tail o' the Pup, 311 N. La Cienega Boulevard (currently located at 329 North San Vincente Boulevard), 1946. *Bottom*. Opening of the Tail o'

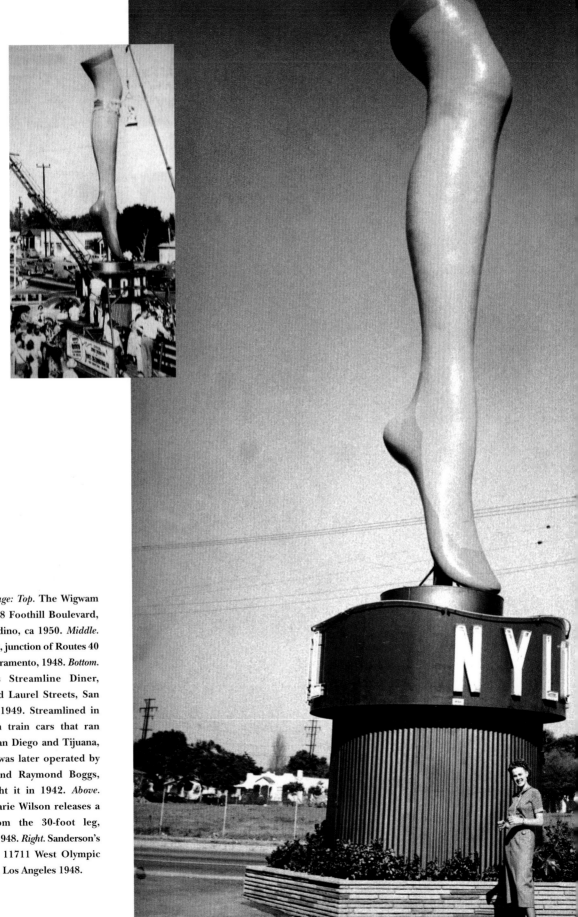

Opposite page: Top. The Wigwam Motel, 2728 Foothill Boulevard, San Bernadino, ca 1950. *Middle.* Capitol Inn, junction of Routes 40 and 99, Sacramento, 1948. *Bottom.* Friedhof's Streamline Diner, Pacific and Laurel Streets, San Diego, ca 1949. Streamlined in 1935 from train cars that ran between San Diego and Tijuana, the diner was later operated by Herbert and Raymond Boggs, who bought it in 1942. *Above.* Actress Marie Wilson releases a garter from the 30-foot leg, February, 1948. *Right.* Sanderson's Stockings, 11711 West Olympic Boulevard, Los Angeles 1948.

Opposite. The Big Donut, Manchester Avenue and La Cienega Boulevard and various locations throughout Southern California, 1950. Owner: Russ Wendell. *This page: Top.* Theodore's School of Music, 1666 Union Street, San Francisco, 1950. Owner: Theodore Pezzolo. *Above.* Santa Claus, California, Highway 101, Carpenteria, 1948. Designer: Pat McKeon. Owners: Ruth and Hap Schaergus.

Opposite page: Top. Beany's Drive-In, Long Beach, ca 1955. *Bottom.* Curries Ice Cream. Various locations throughout Los Angeles, ca 1953. *Above.* The Barrel Club, 404 Lincoln Highway No. 40 at Benicia Road, Vallejo, ca 1948. Owners: The Curtola Brothers. *Left.* The Dog House, original location 1270 North Vermont Avenue, Los Angeles, 1963.

Top. Doggie Diner, various locations in the Bay Area, ca 1948. *Bottom.* Pickle Bill's, 2714 Pico Boulevard, Santa Monica, ca 1948. *Opposite page: Top.* Deschwanden's Shoe Repair, Chester and 10th Streets, Bakersfield, 1947. *Bottom.* The Donut Hole, 15300 Amar Road, La Puente, 1969. Architect: E. Forestal.

A revival of the California Crazy concept produced these contemporary examples during the 1980s and 1990s. *Opposite page: Top.* The Showboat, 3242 Cahuenga Boulevard, Los Angeles, 1968. *Bottom.* The Shutter Shack, 15336 Golden West Street, Westminster, 1977. Owner and designer: Susan Bel Monte. *This page: Top left.* Team Disney Building, Disney Studios, Burbank, 1990. Architect: Michael Graves. *Top right.* Fleetwood Square, 19611 Ventura Boulevard, Woodland Hills, 1987. *Bottom left.* The Hamburger That Ate L.A., 7600 Melrose Avenue, 1989. *Bottom right.* Chiat Day advertising agency, 340 Main Street, Venice, 1991. Architect: Frank Gehry.

Above. **The Big Duck, Long Island, New York, ca 1931. Original owner: Martin Maurer. Designed by William Collins and built by Smith & Yeager. Now located at Sears-Bellow County Park, Route 24, Flanders, New York.** *Opposite page: Top.* **The Coffee Pot, New Bedford, Pennsylvania, ca 1928.** *Middle.* **Ice Cream Cannister, New Jersey, ca 1933.** *Bottom.* **Indian Village, Lawrence, Kansas, May 30, 1930. Owner: F. W. McDonald.**

CHAPTER 2

OUT-OF-STATE ODDITIES

For the better part of the twentieth century, California could confidently proclaim itself the crazy-building capital of the world by virtue of the sheer concentration of its nonconformist architecture. But that exclusive title was diminished somewhat when a survey of oddball buildings across the United States was considered. Despite the favorable weather, expansive urban areas, and commitment to the automobile, California's architectural aberrations were joined by thousands more along roadsides, in cities, over hinterlands, and across the breadth of America.

You can attribute this building boom to the automobile. The introduction of Henry Ford's Model T democratized the ownership of a car. Between 1909 and 1926—the life span of the Model T—the number of cars on the highway went from 300,000 to over 20 million. The proliferation of twentieth-century buildings that were constructed to look like apples, pigs, kettles, grasshoppers, and the like were a direct product of this emerging car culture, which accelerated in the late teens and early twenties. Initially, the automobile, which was born in Europe, was slower in acceptance on American shores. But once embraced, enthusiasm for this new type of transportation was unbridled. A mobile American public, which had a vast countryside to explore by automobile, was a potent force in pushing businesses to seek new ways to address and advertise products. One solution to this dilemma was to create businesses that could not be ignored by a customer driving at thirty-five miles per hour. Bolstered by examples from other sectors of the architectural environment, most notably the contained grounds of amusement parks and expositions, business owners throughout the

United States began creating wildly imaginative structures to entice customers. Adding to this atmosphere was the giddy climate of the post–World War I period. What became known as the Roaring Twenties was in fact an economic boom and social revolution against conservative values. The ability to defy convention and try things out of the ordinary further fueled the building of the bizarre.

Predating this surge of building activity before the automobile was a fixture on American roads, several giant elephants grabbed the public's attention on the East Coast. "Lucy," a ninety-ton behemoth, was constructed in 1881 in Margate, New Jersey as a real estate promotion. The brainchild of James Vincente de Paul Lafferty, an engineer, inventor,

Above. **Lucy the Elephant, Margate, New Jersey, 1881.** *Opposite page.* **Various examples of large-scale advertising structures, European style. (1 & 2) Booths at the Leipzig Trade Fair, 1927. (3) A birdcage constructed out of neon for a Paris department store, 1927. (4) Advertising building at a Swedish Exposition, 1907.**

and real estate investor, Lucy served as an advertising device and novelty for visitors to the beachfront property. She was joined several years later by the Colossal Elephant of Coney Island (1884), another massive structure built and designed by J. Mason Kirby of Atlantic City, New Jersey. While this building was intended as a hotel, it eventually became a concert hall and tourist attraction. Constructed entirely of wood, the 150-foot-long by 88-foot-high structure was capped by an observation howdah. The thirty-four rooms in the structure were dominated by the grand hall, which was entered by the stomach room via staircases installed in the legs. To further amaze visitors, promoters provided sightseers with a list of pachyderm statistics. The elephant was sheathed in 35,000 square feet of tin, weighed 100,000 tons, contained 1,500,000 square feet of lumber, and required 7 tons of bolts and 700 kegs of nails to complete. Two years later, the elephantine colossus was destroyed by a fire. A third elephant, the Light of Asia, was constructed at South Cape May, New Jersey, but it too disappeared by the early 1900s.

Beyond displaying newfound engineering skills, many of these early prototype buildings focused on the advertising value that could be extracted from them. Their sedentary nature made them more of an architec-

tural folly that addressed no specific consumer need. The next generation of novel buildings would directly speak to the commercial marketplace via the automobile.

Paralleling the rise of these unconventional commercial buildings were various residences that appropriated imagery from exotic and unusual sources. The appropriation of exoticism wasn't a new concept; homeowners had been creating replicas of palaces and castles for hundreds of years. The affordability of the single-family dwelling in the early part of the twentieth century made it feasible for the middle class to further pursue their fantasies on a mass scale. By adopting European and Asian influences or constructing their homes in various period revival styles, many homeowners sought to imbue their domiciles with a hint of the past or at least to replicate another era or land. For some that was not enough. Many individuals took domestic architecture to edgier extremes, thereby letting their personal muse run rampant with some absurd home

expressions. This exotic building type, while not commercial in nature, was once again indicative of a climate that allowed for the spirited expression and construction of the many odd commercial buildings that were to be built.

A motorized society that was in full swing by the 1920s began to put demands on architecture to utilize this emerging vehicle. Gasoline stations and motels were a specific response to this new car culture. Soon, however, restaurants, markets, movie theaters, and shopping centers began to be designed and constructed to meet the demands of a newly mobile public. While this accelerated rate of building construction was more evident in California, where wide-open spaces and affordable land for development were more readily available in a defined area, the highways and byways across the country were soon consumed with a similar building boom as lunch stands, roadside stops, ser-

vice stations, and the like clambered for attention and the motorist's dollar. This informal building upsurge saw programmatic examples proliferating in a direct response to the speed with which consumers were passing their buildings. Built by a range of individuals, from accomplished architects to novice construction workers with no formal training, roadside architecture was soon seeing giant icebergs, sombreros, and oversized ice cream cartons in a parade of the impossible. By the mid-twenties these buildings were hitting their stride.

As navigable roads increased, so did the roadside businesses that catered to the ever-growing wanderlust of the American public. In America, the best

Above. **Nehi gas station, Opelika, Alabama, 1924.** *Opposite page: Top.* **Bond drive promotion, the "U Buy A Bond" submarine in Central Park, New York City, 1916.** *Bottom.* **The battleship "Recruit" in Union Square, New York City, 1918.**

examples of the programmatic took place in the late twenties and early thirties. The more obvious services catering to highway enthusiasts—gas stations, cafes, motels, and roadside attractions—readily accepted programmatic dressings. In addition to the predictable windmills, milk bottles, and so on, there were exceptions: A giant Nehi soft drink bottle called the Twist Inn (1924) caught early travelers' attention near Opelika, Alabama. Tourists could climb up the neck of the bottle, which served as an observation post. The Popcorn Ball and the Golf Ball, two moveable food stands, were simple in design but stood out along the highway. The Stump Cafe (ca 1934) in Texarkana, a cluster of stucco tree stumps, was a different take on the well-worn log theme. The crudely constructed Fish Inn (ca 1930) in Coeur d'Alene, Idaho bordered on folk art with its scales made of shingles. The Big Duck, made of secondhand lumber and concrete in 1931, was a salesroom for Long Island duck farmer Martin Maurer, who constructed a wonderful specimen of vernacular art. Wadhams Service Station (ca 1929) in Milwaukee took an entirely different slant on gas station imagery by making the station complex a Chinese pagoda—office and work bays included. The A&W Indian-head root beer stand (ca 1934) was a nice alternative to the chain's familiar giant root beer barrels.

Many businesses that maintained franchises or chains used less-invasive imagery to sell their product. Stands such as White Castle and White Tower effectively used the image of a medieval European castle to draw attention to their hamburger businesses. This approach, while novel, was not as startling as the sight of an oversized animal or product. These buildings created a similar response by offering the public something out of the ordinary but with an image that was familiar. This tendency in some programmatic architecture to draw attention in a less demonstrative manner saw recurring themes emerge. Based in part on the simplicity of form and ease of construction, imagery that was familiar to read yet different enough to be noticed resulted in multiple versions of windmills, barrels, teapots, and teepees. Nautical motifs also abounded and slews of boats, ocean liners, ships, and lighthouses could be found near

Top. **Moxie Bottle, Pine Island Park, Manchester, New Hampshire, ca 1910.** *Bottom.* **Giant Cash Register, bond drive promotion, Dayton, Ohio, 1918.**

bodies of water and along landlocked roadways. Another popular image was that of the Western frontier, which produced log cabins, covered wagons, trading posts, forts, hundreds of wigwam motor courts, refreshment stands, dance halls, and whatever else the image of the Indian could invoke and sell.

The widely published examples of late 1920s and early 1930s programmatic architecture in California invited owners from other states to liberally borrow designs. In Kansas another Brown Derby restaurant stood forlornly on the plains in contrast to its urban namesake. A Big Freezer ice cream stand similar to the ones spread across Los Angeles was built on the highway between Morrison and Denver, Colorado. Ann's Shoe Tavern, a Mother Goose–inspired restaurant in the shape of a shoe near Ogden, Utah, was built several years after the original Pasadena, California version. Whether it was pure coincidence or pure imitation, California buildings impacted some of what was being built in the rest of the country.

While California prompted programmatic inspiration on a national scale, it didn't hold the exclusive rights to the tradition of period revivals. Long ingrained as an architectural device, the borrowing and transposing of foreign styles including Egyptian, Islamic, European, and Asian influences continued apace for commercial buildings. Fraternal organizations with their mysterious and often clandestine rites were grand proponents of Middle Eastern designs. Shriner mosques and Masonic Egyptian halls infused a bit of the exotic to a sometimes mundane town. Movie theaters also exploited this illusionistic world by taking customers out of the everyday life and placing them in fantasy environments. Selective regions were also mined for historic references. The Colonial Style, heavily utilized on the Eastern seaboard, represented a clean, conservative, and classical image making that was easily adopted for everything from restaurants to hotels. In the Southwest, the Pueblo Style was used in much the same way to reference a sometimes accurate history; at other times it dissolved into kitsch. In addition to commercial enterprises, many civic buildings, particularly in New Mexico, took their architectural cues from local indigenous

Top. **The Castle Inn, New York, 1928.** *Middle.* **The Ship dance hall, Fort Worth, Texas, 1928.** *Bottom.* **Sphinx gas station, 1932.**

cultures. Florida's real estate splurge in the twenties and the resulting boom and bust produced some wildly imaginative domestic and commercial buildings in the Mediterranean and Spanish styles in a nod to the state's history and climate. In a movement that paralleled California's, developers leaned on the exaggerated and fantastic to sell lots and commercial districts fashioned after Italian- and Middle Eastern–inspired designs.

By the mid-1930s, the streamlining of America and the introduction of Modernism effectively changed the way people began to view popular architecture. The Streamline Moderne Style conjured up cleanliness, speed, efficiency, and the future—attributes admired in a period of economic depression. At Chicago's Century of Progress exposition in 1933 and later at the 1939 New York World's Fair, a full range of buildings in the Streamline Moderne Style was introduced to an admiring public. Once absorbed into the mainstream, this new style dominated commercial buildings, and the roadside "novelty" building began to be viewed as old-fashioned. Still, a large

Opposite page: Top. **Polks Dairy, Indianapolis, Indiana, 1921.** *Middle.* **Asselin Creamery, Norway, Indiana, ca 1929.** *Bottom.* **Halifax Creamery, Daytona, Florida, ca 1932.** *Below.* **Freda Farms, Berlin, Connecticut, 1933.**

segment of the mobile public found the roadside buildings appealing landmarks with their implied humor and guileless oversized message. Eventually a few programmatic buildings adopted the Streamline Moderne Style, usually by mimicking transportation models such as trains or ocean liners. But even with this temporary design diversion, it became clear that the runaway building of programmatic structures had begun to wane.

World War II put a momentary hold on programmatic construction. The unavailability of building materials plus the rationing of gas, which severely limited travel, inhibited what already was a fading architectural form. The war effort did accelerate new technologies that would later provide materials for future, large-scale signs and sculpture, but for the duration of the war most of these buildings languished.

With the rise of the interstate highway construction in the postwar period, Americans were once again on the road. For the most part, the highway retained a programmatic presence. To be sure, larger cities and towns had their share of unusual buildings, but the expectations of travelers for roadside anomalies made this type of building most viable on the open road. In an ironic twist, the expanding interstate system would eventually bypass and replace many of the old roads, thus further

diluting a once-thriving roadside culture and eliminating what was left of those early structures on main highways.

The slow pace of programmatic building in the late 1930s continued after the war, with a few outstanding examples joining those already on the scene. The Haines Shoe House near York, Pennsylvania (1948), was guest house and advertisement for a shoe store owner. Across the country a couple of ex-GIs built Seattle's Hat n' Boots service station (1947), where you could gas up under the hat rim and relieve yourself in one of the giant boot restrooms. At around the same time, in the middle of the Nevada desert, Las Vegas was beginning to erupt. Las Vegas promised a whole new type of programmatic experience. Here a few of the classic programmatic models would be built, but it was the sign that would be developed, enlarged, and exaggerated beyond previous roadside expectations for future roadside consumption.

Throughout the fifties and sixties a range of buildings, signs, and three-dimensional figures would continue to serve as symbols of an all-inclusive "pop architecture." Included in this catch-all phrase were roadside stands and attractions, exuberant defenders of the programmatic: giant cobras, cheese slices, two-story oranges, castles, molded plastic beasts, insects, produce, dinosaurs, and water towers in various shapes and colors.

Above. **Cowboy hat souvenir stand, Wickenburg, Arizona, ca 1934.** *Opposite page: Top.* **The Wigwam, Adrian, Michigan, ca 1932.** *Bottom.* **The Indian Village, Kansas, ca 1937.**

The Wigwam

In the seventies, the process of reexamining the architectural past began in earnest. Prompted by the quick dissolution of twentieth-century vernacular architecture, preservation groups formed to save and draw attention to a heritage of roadside architecture. Critics, too, began to examine the legacy of the "strip" and how it applied to contemporary architecture. This renewed interest produced a flood of new images and a body of literature that further exposed the depth of commercial and roadside architecture. Inspired by this new awareness, buildings, cued by images from the past, began to take shape.

The participation in the 1990s of established and name architects using programmatic elements raised roadside sensibilities to a new level. By absorbing and translating the past, architects created a new language of the vernacular. Among these structures is Stanley Tigerman's facade (1986) for a twelve-story parking structure in Chicago, which relies on the nostalgia of a 1930s touring car. The architects Michael Graves, Robert A. M. Stern, and Arata Isozaki, and firms such as Arquitectonica were commissioned by the Disney Company to create a range of spirited buildings including a new studio headquarters, resorts, and amusement parks that reinterpreted the vernacular and fostered the culture of entertainment. In an odd way the stepchild of "real architecture" has by default been legitimized through the rise of programmatic architecture.

In a development that was impossible to predict, the legacy of twentieth-century roadside vernacular architecture landed in Las Vegas where the gambling capital has produced the ultimate roadside fantasy. Abandoning the engorged neon sign

This page: Top to bottom. **The borrowings of exotic styles and modifications of regional architecture resulted in a nationwide building splurge of period revival structures. The Tripoli Temple Shrine Mosque, Milwaukee, Wisconsin, ca 1934. Masonic Temple, Racine, Wisconsin, ca 1930. The Coliseum, St. Petersburg, Florida, ca 1928. Kimo Theatre, Albuquerque, New Mexico, 1927. The Log Cabin Inn, Ocean Boulevard, Atlantic Highlands, New Jersey, ca 1930.** *Opposite page: Top to bottom.* **One of the more common expressions of the programmatic, windmills could be found in a variety of situations and locations. The Windmill, Route 6, Laceyville, Pennsylvania, ca 1935. The Windmill tourist camp, tea room, and gas station, Seneca Falls, New York, ca 1927.**

Left. The William Penn Diner, U.S. Routes 13 and 40, six miles south of Wilmington, Delaware, ca 1939. *Crossover.* The Red Apple grocery store and gas station, Wichita, Kansas, ca 1933. *Opposite.* Ann's Shoe Tavern, Ogden, Colorado, ca 1935. Owner: Mrs. Fleming.

that had dominated the strip, casinos produced a bizarre, hopped-up-on-steroids main street in the nineties. Now Roman palaces and pirate ships fight for customers' attention along with multistory jukeboxes, Coke bottles, gargantuan pharaohs, immensely scaled pyramids, fantasy castles, and a giant, golden lion's head. Seventy years later a drive down "main street" at thirty-five miles per hour has taken on a new meaning.

With a new century ahead, the future development of roadside vernacular architecture is open for all sorts of architectural meanderings and interpretations. If the checkered history of the programmatic experience—from advertising elephants to modest roadside stands to corporate buildings—is any indication of the future, the evolution of this intriguing style of architecture will be fascinating to follow.

Top. Kid Blair's Showboat, Route 3, on Lake Tiogue, Washington, Rhode Island, ca 1936. *Above*. Showboat Drive-In Theater, Highway 10, Coeur d' Alene, Idaho, ca 1946. *Opposite page: Top*. Vico Gas Station, Salt Lake City, Utah, ca 1924. *Middle*. Weismantel's Showboat, 808-20 Jamaica Avenue, Cypress Hills, New York, ca 1936. *Bottom*. George A. Simpson Lunchboat, ca 1932.

Opposite page: Top. **The Cider Barrel, Ballincara Orchard, Germantown, Minnesota, ca 1939.** *Bottom.* **The Cider Barrel, Gaithesburg, Maryland, ca 1939.** *Above left.* **The Pickle Barrel, Grand Marais, Michigan, ca 1926.** *Above right.* **Indian head root beer stand, 38th and State Avenue, Kansas City, Kansas.** *Below.* **A&W Root Beer Stand, 2710 W. Broadstreet, Richmond, Virginia, ca 1931.**

Opposite page: Top. The Fish Inn, Coeur d' Alene, Idaho, ca 1930. *Bottom.* Striper No. 1 Fish Stand, Rio Vista, California, 1934. Owner: H. J. Howden. *Above.* The Pig Barbecue, Harlington, Texas, ca 1939. *Below.* The Big Fish, Peninsula Park, Erie, Pennsylvania, ca 1935.

Opposite. The Dog, U.S. 99 near Lane, Oregon, 1935. *Below.* The Melon Patch, Portland, Oregon, ca 1930.

World's fairs and expositions provided the perfect environment for entertainment and fantasy architecture. *Opposite page: Top.* Cobb's Chicken House, Golden Gate International Exposition, San Francisco, 1939–40. *Middle.* Little America, Texas Centennial Exposition, Dallas, 1936. *Bottom.* Enchanted Island, Century of Progress, Chicago, 1933–34. *This page: Top left.* The World a Million Years Ago, Century of Progress, Chicago, 1933–34. *Top right.* Shell Oil Company, California Pacific International Exposition, San Diego, 1935. Architect: L. Raymond White. *Bottom.* Streets of Paris, Century of Progress, Chicago, 1933–34.

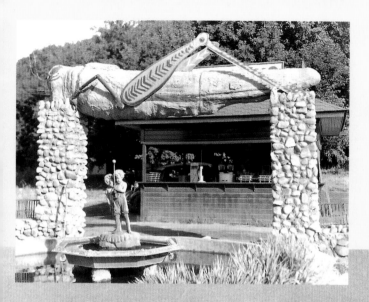

Left. The Grasshopper Root Beer Stand, Riverdale Road, Ogden, Utah, 1931. *Below.* Goody Goody Coffee Pot, location unknown.

Right. The Big Red Apple, Highway 36, Wathena, Kansas, ca 1929. *Below.* Ocean Spray Cranberry Cocktail bottle, Route 6 and 28, Onset, Massachusetts, October 1947.

Top. Art Ware Teapot, Chester, West Virginia, ca 1939. *Middle.* The Orange Box, U.S. Highway 17, Winterhaven, Florida, ca 1936. *Bottom.* Dairyland, Boston-Worcester Turnpike, Shrewsbury, Massachusetts, ca 1937.

Top. The Lobster Trap, location unknown, ca 1949. *Middle.* Walt's Restaurant, U.S. Highway 46, Essex County, New Jersey, July 1947. *Bottom.* Petrified Wood Gas Station, Lamar, Colorado, ca 1935.

Above. The Coffee Pot, Highway 31, Austin, Indiana, 1929. Original owner: J. G. Bennett. *Left.* Sisson's Coffee Pot, Port Malobar, Florida, ca 1938. *Opposite page: Top.* The Big Pump, Highway 71, Maryville, Maryland, ca 1937. *Bottom.* The Barge, East Washington and Denny Streets, Indianapolis, Indiana, 1935. *Following Spread.* The Iceberg, near Albuquerque, New Mexico, ca 1941.

Above. Charlie's Diner, Richmond Road, Pennsylvania, ca 1944. *Below.* Wigwam Motel, Horse Cave, Kentucky, 1936. Original owner: F. A. Radford. *Opposite page: Top.* Noah's Ark, U.S. Highway 27, Sunbright, Tennessee, ca 1936. *Bottom.* Polar Bear Frozen Custard, Central and Oliver Streets, Wichita, Kansas, 1938.

Opposite page: Top and middle. Coon Chicken Inn, 2950 Highland Drive, Salt Lake City, Utah, 1924. *Bottom.* Mammy's Cupboard, Natchez, Mississippi, ca 1946. Original owner: Henry Gaude. *This page: Top left.* The Derby Drive-In, Henderson, Kentucky, ca 1935. *Top right.* Brown Derby Cottages Inc., Evansville, Indiana, ca 1935. *Bottom.* The Sombrero, "El Charro," San Pedro Villa de Santiago, Nuevo Laredo, Monterrey, Mexico, ca 1938.

APE HICKORY TAVERN
HY-WAY NO. 10-70
3 MILES WEST of HICKORY

Opposite page: Top. Cape Hickory Tavern, Highway 10-70, Hickory, location unknown, ca 1939. *Middle.* Airplane Service Station, Highways 219 and 8, Rich Creek, Virginia, ca 1938. Original owner: O. L . Spangler. *Bottom.* Bodles Freezer, Route 15, Williamsport, Pennsylvania, ca 1942. *Above.* The Stump Cafe, Highway 59, Texarkana, Texas, ca 1933. *Below.* Wadhams Service Station No. 27, 27th Street and Wisconsin Avenue, Milwaukee, Wisconsin, ca 1930, originally built 1917.

Opposite page: Top. The Miner's Hat, Interstate 90, Kellog, Idaho, 1940. Original owner: Mary Etta Page. *Bottom.* The Bomber Service Station, Highway 99, south of Portland, Oregon, ca 1947. *Above.* El Sombrero Drive-In, Route 66, Albuquerque, New Mexico, 1948. *Below.* Hat n' Boots Service Station, East Marginal Way and Carson, Seattle, Washington, 1947.

Above. The Food Basket, location unknown, ca 1958. *Below.* Wing Co. television store, 1041 East Colorado Boulevard, Pasadena, California, ca 1951.

Above. **Dilly-Wagon Drive-In, location unknown, ca 1962.** *Below.* **World's Largest Covered Wagon, Interstate 80, Exit 382, Milford, Nebraska, 1976. Owner: Kenneth Dahle.**

This page: Top. The Shoe House, Route 30 East, York, Pennsylvania, 1948. Original owner: Mahlon Haines. *Middle*. Miami Serpentarium, Miami, Florida, ca 1965. *Bottom*. U.S. Royal Giant Tire, New York World's Fair, 1964. *Opposite page: Top*. Coney Island Hot Dog, Aspen Park, Colorado, 1966. Original owner: Marcus Shannon. *Middle*. The Cheese House, Arlington, Vermont, ca 1968. *Bottom*. Orange World, 5395 West Bronson Memorial Highway, U.S. Highway 192, Kissimmee, Florida, ca 1982.

Above. Leaning Tower Y.M.C.A., Niles, Illinois, ca 1971. *Below.* Ma Perkins Chicken Inn, U.S. 422 between Niles and Warren, Ohio, ca 1956. *Opposite page: Top.* Dino Service Station, Weeki Wachi Springs, Florida, 1964. *Bottom.* Tomahawk, Cut Knife, Saskatchewan, Canada, 1971.

159

Above. Billings Brewing Company advertising car, Milwaukee, Wisconsin, ca 1920. *Opposite page: Top.* "Wandover Will," the largest mechanical-cowboy sign in the world, State Line Hotel, Route 40-50, Wandover, Nevada, ca 1946. *Middle.* Dinosaur Park, Rapid City, South Dakota, ca 1950. Built by Emmett Sullivan. *Bottom.* World's largest Buffalo, Jamestown, North Dakota, ca 1956.

SIGNS, CARS, AND GIANTS

The drive to create something just a little bit larger, to overstep the boundaries of convention, to excite and surprise, seems to be part of the indomitable human spirit. The Colossus of Rhodes, the Sphinx, the Statue of Liberty, Mount Rushmore, and other examples of gigantic statuary were ways of communicating with higher powers, ways of honoring causes or individuals and celebrating accomplishments. The giant men and oversized signs that continue to be found along American roadways and urban centers are of the same spirit but hold none of the same pretensions. Cultural clutter or vernacular expression, roadside blight or guileless Americana, Pop art or folk art, whatever the category, advertising was the game for the most part, especially when the automobile was factored into the equation. With their ability to gain customers' attention, these Goliaths of the monument and advertising world functioned in much the same manner as billboards except that they grabbed you with a minimal amount of text and a colossal size.

As substitutes for more ambitious and expensive building programs, statues of giant men and women were the perfect solution for businesses and municipalities with more modest expense accounts. For towns looking to attract visitors and tourists, a monument of colossal proportions that paid tribute to some aspect of local commerce or history often brought additional revenue to the area. The almost inexhaustible ranges of these beasts, fruits, vegetables, men, and women of the historical and mythological past are a testament to homespun creativity and that undefinable drive that keeps their construction on a steady course.

One of the earlier attempts at formalizing this tradition was the creation of Paul Bunyan and Babe the Blue Ox at Bemidji, Minnesota (1937). Born out of a devastating winter in Depression-era Minnesota, this thinly veiled advertising gimmick was an accompaniment to a winter carnival. The striking image of a brightly painted folk hero on the barren Midwestern plains was an effective device to get travelers to stop. It became the nexus of what was to become a flourishing regional tradition. Where California succeeded in producing an inordinate amount of outlandish roadside buildings, the Midwest seems to have cornered the colossus market more recently. Mallards, otters, prairie chickens, pelicans, and buffalo have joined corn, shoes, Amish folk, Vikings, frontiersmen, and dinosaurs in a neverending cavalcade of the superlative and bizarre. Across the border, Canadians have aggressively built similar monuments in extension of this concept. You can attribute it to pent-up winter boredom, advertising one-upmanship, or an extension of individualistic frontier spirit. Whatever the cause, these counterpoints to the flat and monotonous plains continue to contribute to the lure of the roadside.

Many of the early examples of oversized statues were usually homemade and of a folk-art nature.

This page: Top. **Vulcan, Birmingham, Alabama Fairgrounds, 1933. Built in 1904 for the Columbian Exposition.** *Bottom.* **Giant Jesus at Gethsemane Church, 1936 patent drawing.** *Opposite page: Top.* **Paul Bunyan, Bimidji, Minnesota, ca 1937.** *Bottom.* **Largest Viking in the World, Alexandria, Minnesota, date unknown.**

Such was the case of the dinosaur at Creston, South Dakota. Using the nearby discovery of dinosaur remains as inspiration, the owners of a local store constructed their roadside attraction in 1933 with a frame of recycled metal which they covered with chicken wire and coated with a veneer of concrete. The same went for the fifteen-foot Bemidji Paul Bunyan (1937), which was constructed by locals in a similarly simplified manner. Until new materials were introduced, the bulk of these creations continued to be built out of available and traditional building supplies. By the early 1950s, fiberglass had become a more common and adaptable material. Used in the customizing of cars (the early Corvette being a prime example), boat hulls, and other products, fiberglass was versatile, pliable, and long lasting—perfect for the construction of giant objectsigns. California inherited much of this postwar technology from the aircraft industry. When the aircraft technology was pressed into other commercial areas, small, local manufacturing firms began to fabricate these roadside giants in the late 1950s and 1960s. The names and origins of many of these companies have been lost, but other figure production firms have attributed some of their early molds to California. One intriguing story gives moldmaking credit to the camouflaging efforts during World War II. Three-dimensional farm animals were produced and mounted on the roofs of aircraft plants. They were disguised to resemble rural landscapes from above. The molds were later bought by a firm making fiberglass figures in North Carolina.

The ubiquitous Muffler Man and its many mutations was the perfect form for molding. These fiberglass men, fashioned into a variety of standardized figures, had interchangeable legs, arms, and heads and could be configured for a broad variety of appearances. The most common designs were a Paul Bunyan–inspired lumberjack, a cowboy, an Indian, and a service-station attendant. Found throughout California, the statues spread to the rest of the country by happenstance and customer request. One California manufacturer reportedly made the Bunyan giant for the 1964–65 New York World's Fair and later marketed the statue at tire conventions, which accounts for the predominance of the giants at auto-related locations and hence the name Muffler Men. Steve Dashew's Venice, California fiberglass company made a similar claim of having created a Paul Bunyan figure

Top, left to right. **Muffler Men: Babe's Mufflers, San Jose; used car lot, Los Angeles, ca 1978; Tom's Steak and Hoagies, Edgewater, New Jersey, ca 1976.** *Left.* **Ali Baba's, Hollywood, ca 1976.**

for a Phoenix restaurateur in 1964, thereby jump-starting the manufacture of giants, which contin-ued until 1974.

The mobility of the advertising giants has left them with a checkered history. Add the fre-quent modifications that new owners made to the outfits, body parts, and skin color, and the genealogy all but vanishes. A blue-painted Indian advertised tires at a Signal Hill, California tire outlet, while another was painted to resemble an African-American at a nearby car dealership. Both have disappeared. An amusement park Frankenstein has been pieced together from obvious Muffler Man parts in Bridgeview, Illi-nois. Malibu, California is home to a decades-old snack stand that proudly displayed a

counter chef that held a massive hamburger atop its building. The local landmark's fate was on hold as new owners opened a La Salsa Mexi-can food outlet in the space. Acknowledging its significance, the new owners refitted the giant with a sombrero, serape, sandals, and a burrito plate garnished with oversized chiles. The list goes on and on. A phenomenon unto them-selves, these advertising statues have somehow survived several decades of abuse and indiffer-ence, and have maintained their presence on the streets and highways in one of America's more bizarre traditions.

While the aberrant Muffler Men continue to be placemarks across the United States, they have been joined by a new generation of sculpted forms

Top, left to right. **Chicken Boy, Los Angeles, ca 1978. The soda-jerk man stood on top of a food stand in Malibu on Pacific Coast Highway for a good decade or more until it was purchased for a Mexican food outlet, prompting the new owners to re-outfit the fiberglass giant with a sombrero, serape, and huaraches. Transformation, 1990s.** *Right.* **Chief Auto Supply, Signal Hill, ca 1975.**

Custom-designed giants have made their way into every nook and cranny of the United States. The F.A.S.T. (Fiberglass Animals, Shapes, and Trademarks) Corporation of Sparta, Wisconsin is responsible for a large number of objects that grace miniature golf courses, water parks, front yards, and civic plazas. The Jolly Green Giant statue in Blue Earth, Minnesota (1978); the giant, killer bee in Hidalgo, Texas (1992); the twenty-five-foot monkey at the South of the Border tourist stop in South Carolina (ca 1975); and the truckloads of Bob's Big Boy giants are all the creations of owner Jerry Vetrus, who started his business in 1983. His pièce-de-résistance, however, is the 143-foot Muskie, a massive fish created for the National Fresh Water Fishing Hall of Fame in Hayward, Wisconsin in 1979.

In a lighter vein, a current builder of giants, Gary Greff of North Dakota, has sculpted a series of metal figures along the Enchanted Highway, a road that leads into Regent, his hometown. Once a junior high school principal, Greff has crafted a flock of pheasants, the world's largest grasshopper, and a tin family.

Plans are in the works for a series of geese to rise out of the prairie subsidized by donations and grants. All are part of a larger plan to draw visitors to the farming town. More sculptures are scheduled to be built at three-mile intervals along the road. Part sign, part art, the statues straddle the middle ground of the programmatic spectrum.

In a category by themselves, embellished automobiles fall within programmatic guidelines. Unique advertising devices on a par with signs and giants, they are a somewhat limited breed. The automobile as sign presents an odd twist in the world of advertising and the built environment. While most programmatic buildings addressed a mobile public, autos constructed to look like shoes, houses, chickens, or hot dogs became mobile advertising speaking to a mostly stationary audience.

The most creative period for these auto advertisers was in the early years of the automobile. Mostly built in a prolific pre-1930 period, these types of vehicles were still being produced in subsequent decades. With few, if any, guidelines to impinge on their creativity, most anything that could be welded or mounted on a car could be turned into an advertising vehicle. The published examples of most of these vehicles show a high degree of sophistication, which seemed necessary if the product they were advertising were to be viewed positively. Their novel effect often limited production to specialized applications and they remain for the most part one-of-a-kind. The one

exception has been the Oscar Mayer Weinermobile, whose multiple units can still be seen in various parts of the country. Personally decorated or customized cars, which fall outside the boundaries of a programmatic framework, are more the visible counterparts to the advertising vehicle and this phenomenon continues to progress at full speed ahead.

This page: Top left. **The Wild Goose, Wawa, Ontario, Canada, September 1960.** *Bottom left*. **May Museum of the Tropics featuring Dynastes Hercules, the world's largest beetle, Weeki Watchee Spring, Florida, ca 1955.** *Right*. **Largest pheasant in the world, U.S. Highway 14, Huron, South Dakota. Date unknown.** *Opposite page:* **Advertising automobiles were a by-product of a car-crazy America. A cousin to programmatic structures, these cars took their advertising on the road.** *Top to bottom: Left column*. **Autohouse for midget family, ca 1932; camera car, Warren S. O'Brien studios, Waukesha, Wisconsin, ca 1930; Budweiser III land boat, ca 1925; Chicken Dinner Candy Bar car, Milwaukee, Wisconsin, ca 1950.** *Right column*. **Chicken Dinner Candy Bar car, ca 1933; Oertel's Little Brown Jug ale car, ca 1935; Wynn's Airplane Tire delivery, Los Angeles, ca 1930; The Oscar Mayer Weinermobile, ca 1952.**

Above. Six-pack of Corona beer, Baja California, Mexico, 1990. *Opposite page: Top*. Longaberger Basket Company corporate headquarters, Newark, Ohio, 1998. *Middle*. Benewah Dairy Milk Bottle, Post and Garland Streets, Tacoma, Washington, 1934. *Bottom*. Twist o' the Mist, Niagara Falls, New York, 2000.

CHAPTER 4

CURRENT CONDITION

The entrepreneurial desire to create something monumental and memorable has kept the programmatic style alive. Despite the gradual decline of vernacular architecture along the road, the construction of oddly shaped buildings, giant signs, and exaggerated structures and monuments has progressed at a slower pace than in its heyday in the 1920s and 1930s. The range of building possibilities has expanded from highly sophisticated architectural statements to folk art styles. The bulk of these newer buildings in the public sector are usually tamer versions of their counterparts from

the past with the exception being the latest building boomlet in entertainment architecture as produced in Las Vegas and by the Disney Company.

The California Crazy legacy has been left with three levels of participants: the individual artist, the individual business/civic group, and the corporate/entertainment entity. Included in this building evolution are the buildings' new placement within the environment. Once the domain of the highway, roadside architecture has been joined by an increasing number of urban versions, and examples of the amusement park and zone variety. The contemporary substitutes for programmatic buildings—inflatables, giant men, etc.—derive in part from the inability to construct the models of the past and from the many factors inhibiting the return of the classic programmatic building. Chief among these factors are updated building codes that prevent many of the smaller, more whimsical structures of the past from being built today. The days of two-by-fours, chicken wire, and stucco have been replaced by rules governing handicap access, fire prevention, earthquake safety, and signage restriction with the resultant unconventional buildings being more conservative. Yet the corporate headquar-

ters for the Longaberger Basket Company in Ohio (1998) is testament to the inventiveness and structural integrity of the type of buildings that can be built today with the right financing. Today's buildings can at least surpass the old buildings in scale.

Las Vegas is the exception. Las Vegas illustrates the dramatic possibilities of three-dimensional Pop expressions. On a scale hardly envisioned by the modest owners of vintage roadside buildings, Las Vegas has managed to push the boundaries when it comes to creating the bigger and the better. Vegas, which has never been afraid to embrace the outrageous, is showing the rest of the world how far the idea of the building as sign can go. Due to the continual process of transformation, the bar has risen from the early flash of neon walls to the monu-

Top left. **A recent programmatic addition, Pharoah's Lost Kingdom in Redlands, California, appropriated the familiar visual language of Egypt, 1996.** *Top right*. **The California Citrus State Historic Park in Riverside re-created a familiar roadside icon, the giant-orange refreshment stand, 1995.** *Bottom left*. **Premiere promotion for** *Jack Frost*, **Cinerama Dome, Hollywood, 1998.** *Bottom right*. **Fry's Electronics, 2311 Hollywood Way, Burbank, California, 1996.**

mentally scaled kitsch of the Luxor pyramid hotel (1993) rising out of the desert.

Today downtown Las Vegas casinos compete with neon signs, but the early Las Vegas Strip was different. With plenty of highway leading into the Vegas center, resorts and hotels used the exaggerated sign as a way of pulling in customers. The imagery of the Old West, which was well established downtown, was an easy and comfortable sell on the Strip. Like many revivalist periods, the Old West Style often led to more extreme stylings. The Showboat Casino, built in 1954 on Boulder Highway, was one of the earliest casinos to exploit the exaggeration of size and scale. The juxtaposition of a gambling barge in the middle of the desert imbued the building with enough novelty and wry

Top left. **One of three extant Big Donuts from the 1950s, Kindle's Donuts, Century and Normandie, Los Angeles, photo 2000.** *Top right*. **A stylized star logo for a Carl's Jr. fast food restaurant is supported by french fries. Orange, California, 1999.** *Bottom left*. **A knife blade appears to slice the Margo Leavin Gallery in half. West Hollywood, California, ca 1994.** *Bottom right*. **A giant free-standing light bulb does the advertising duties at Stan's Lighting Distribution, 5925 West Pico Boulevard, Los Angeles, 1986.**

humor to draw visitors' attention. In 1955, the Dunes Hotel installed a giant fiberglass man—a two-story sultan that reigned above a porte-cochere. He joined giant object-signs built several years earlier, such as El Rancho Vegas' (1943) neon windmill and a sheet metal Thunderbird for the Thunderbird Hotel (1948). High-rises and massive signs such as the Stardust Hotel's (1958) billboard with its gigantic extruding globe dominated the Strip for the next several decades. In a bid to push Vegas beyond all expectations, the MGM Grand Hotel (1993) ushered in the latest of the mega-casinos. The giant lion's head logo at the casino's entrance was of a startling scale that was unattainable by past roadside standards, and yet the same principles were at play. Across the street the Excalibur Hotel (1990) erected a monumental castle that at once dominated the Strip. In an ongoing game of classic Vegas one-upmanship the Luxor (1993) turned its entire complex into one giant pyramid surrounded by sphinxes and gargantuan pharaohs.

The current Las Vegas is flush with mock palazzos, Southeast-Asian ruins, re-creations of pirates' brigs, and renditions of European capitals. Gigantic Coke bottles, the skyline of Manhattan, massive

guitars, and four-story jukeboxes have taken architecture beyond the roaside and the vernacular into a separate category. The pressure to keep the public interested in something new has created a sort of built-in obsolescence for most of the new casinos. Yet by using this mandate and an unbridled imagination as a guidepost, architects have set the stage for an outrageousness that only Las Vegas can provide.

Upping the ante for corporate sponsorship of out-of-the-ordinary, thematic architecture, the Walt Disney Company, purveyors of the world of make-believe, commissioned a series of architects to design buildings throughout the Disney realm. Michael Graves built the new Team Disney headquarters (1990) in Burbank. Graves added the Seven Dwarfs from Snow White's fairy tale as caryatids supporting the entablature and pediment. On another part of the lot, Robert Stern designed the Feature Animation Building (1995) with sly references to Disney cartoons and animation. Edison Field (1997), a baseball park in Orange County, has used elements of the

Pop vernacular to add a touch of whimsy to the game. Flanking the entry plaza are two enormous baseball caps while above the supporting columns of the entry canopy are a series of giant baseball bats.

At Florida's Disney World, the firm of Arquitectonica included inflated footballs, surfboards, and helmets for the All-Sports-themed resort in a bid to interpret the language of the motel. The adjoining hotels of the Disney World complex were also given varied treatments of Pop sensibilities from a range of architects commissioned by Michael Eisner, head of the Disney Company.

Top left. **The Igloo Lodge, Parke Highway, Alaska Route 3, between Anchorage and Fairbanks, Alaska, 1970. Original owner: Leon Smith.** *Top right.* **United Equipment Company, 600 West Glenwood, Turlock, California, 1976. Original owner: Harold Logsdon. Architect: Cliff Cheney.** *Bottom left.* **The Giant Artichoke, Castroville, California, 1972. Original owner: Ray Gei.** *Bottom right.* **The Bull Stops Here barbecue stand, Route 198 east of Visalia, California, 1998.**

Disney is not alone among entertainment companies that have capitalized on the California Crazy concept of architecture. The CityWalk portion of Universal City Hollywood integrated a giant surfboard for the roof of a retail store and continues to embellish its faux urban street with these types of elements. Some restaurant chains and retail stores, such as Country Star Hollywood with its giant jukebox entrance, have used programmatic imagery to add new variations to the time-honored theme of urban street re-creation as well.

Meanwhile, the highly visible projects produced by entertainment companies and Las Vegas titans

have not deterred others from producing their own personal versions of the programmatic. Although not as ambitious as the deep-pocket ventures of large companies, these new programmatic projects remain true to the basic premise of advertising: amuse viewers and attract attention. The various molded figures that have been so popular in the upper Midwest, the latest giant inflatables, and the ongoing, personal, three-dimensional statements of these new projects promise a healthy future for the programmatic.

While critics vary widely in their opinions of the current crop of programmatic manifestations, what cannot be denied is the programmatic's presence in the American landscape. With imitations springing up throughout the world, these buildings, structures, and signs remain a uniquely American by-product. They add yet another footnote to the history of architecture and provide a placemark for personal memories while revealing much about the American psyche.

Top left. **National Fishing Hall of Fame, Haywood, Wisconsin. 1979.** *Top right.* **Dinosaur Gardens, Cabazon, California. Started in 1967 by Claude Bell, who was inspired to build his creations by childhood memories of the Lucy the Margate elephant.** *Bottom left.* **Originally The Big Horn Restaurant, Amado, Arizona, ca 1975.** *Bottom right.* **Alien Flying Saucer at the Tower Mart convenience store, Lathrop, California, ca 1999.**

Top left. The MGM Grand sports a gaudy version of its logo in a massive, golden, lion entrance, 1993. *Top right.* In a modest bid to be different, the Showboat Casino, built in 1954, was an early Las Vegas attempt at a programmatic building. *Above left.* The Nevada landing appears as a desert mirage with two land-locked showboats permanently anchored in the sand. Nevada State Line, 1993. *Above right.* Raising the bar, the Luxor casino created an Egyptian fantasy only possible in Las Vegas, 1993. *Below.* A giant Sultan stands guard over the Dunes Casino, 1956.

Preservation is a dicey business. What is and what isn't historical can be debated ad infinitum. Unfortunately, for many of the buildings in this book, their perceived lack of historical value deemed them worthy of benign neglect and demolition. For over half a century, critics and the architectural establishment universally dismissed unconventional roadside architecture as ephemeral and a blight on the landscape, an attitude which reinforced their disposal. The buildings themselves often presented a preservation problem. Built on the premise of short-term usage, they were usually constructed of inexpensive materials that would last a decade or so with proper maintenance. If a business flourished it was either enlarged and remodeled or moved to another location where a more substantial building could be built. In the case of Southern California, potential land usage made many sites transitory so their eventual demise was presumed. In other parts of the country, commercial buildings were given little thought as to their architectural importance until late in the 20th century when preservationists and historical societies began to see value in the recent past. By that time, many of the signature buildings with a programmatic past had disappeared.

There remain some stalwarts out there clinging to their existence by strong lobbying efforts or by dumb luck. Several have been the victim of misguided preservation attempts by owners attempting to infuse a nostalgic representation on an authentic building. In an odd twist on reality several buildings have been reconstructed in contained environments or behind theme park walls. The Bull Dog Cafe for instance was rebuilt (to earthquake standards) inside of the Petersen Automobile Museum in Los Angeles and another version was installed as a static prop at a Disney theme park. But for those structures in the real world, it's a fragile existence. Even in this enlightened age no building out there is immune to the wrecking ball. While the success stories are many, a vigilant eye is still required to ensure that some of these remaining key visual components of commercial American life remain with us.

Then and Now. Programmatic structures that have withstood the test of time. (1) The Fruit Basket, a roadside stand that managed to last forty-five years on Venice Boulevard near La Brea Avenue, Los Angeles. (2) The 1929 Samson Tire Works was transposed into a developer-sensitive remodel in the 1990s. (3) Originally built in the 1920s, the boat apartments in the 700 block of Third Street in Encinitas, California, are still available for rent. (4) The original Irvin Willat Studio was transplanted from Culver City to Beverly Hills in the early 1930s, where it

Index

A

A & W Root Beer Stand, 118, 128, 131
Aimee Semple McPherson's mansion, 46–47
Airplane Cafe, 50
Airplane Service Station, 150–151
The Alessandro Hotel, 42, 52–53
Alexandria Theater, 70
Alhambra Theater, 70
Ali Baba's, 164
Alice Faye's Club Car Restaurant, 15
Angelus Abbey, 46–47, 55
Ann's Shoe Tavern, 119, 126–127
Art Ware Teapot, 139–140
Asselin Creamery, 120–121
Aztec Hotel, 14, 38–39, 50, 52

B

Babe's Mufflers, 164
The Barge, 142–143
Barkies Sandwich Shops, 16, 62, 72
Barn in the Form of a Cow, 8, 9
Barrel Cafe, 45
Barrel Club, 107
The Barrel Inn, 30–31
The Barrell, 128, 130
Beanie and Cecil's, 76
Beany's drive-in, 106–107
The Betsy Ann Ice Cream Outlet, 18–19
Beverly Theatre, 14
The Big Cone, 36–37, 46
Big Donut, 15, 79–80, 104–105, 171
The Big Duck, 112, 118
The Big Fireplace, 32–33
The Big Fish, 133
The Big Freezer, 13, 46, 50, 119
Big Horn Restaurant, 173
The Big Pump, 142–143
The Big Red Apple, 138–139
Big Red Piano, 63, 80
Billings Brewing Company, 160
The Black Tent, 46–47
Bob's Airmail Service, 82–83

Bob's Big Boy, 165
Bodles Freezer, 150–151
The Bomber Service Station, 152–153
Brown Derby Cafe, 15, 16, 63, 90–91, 119
Brown Derby Cottages Inc., 149
Bucket, 67
Budweiser III land boat, 166–167
The Bull Stops Here, 172
The Bulldog Cafe, 60–61, 63, 175

C

Cabot's Old Indian Pueblo, 52–53
Cabrillo, 15
California Citrus State Historic Park, 170
California Corrugated Culvert Company, 10
California Piano Supply Co., 80
Calmos #1 Service Station, 14, 44–45
The Calpet Super Service Station, 47, 55, 62
Calpet's Service Station, 14
Cape Hickory Tavern, 150–151
Capitol Inn, 76, 102–103
Carl's Jr., 171
Carthay Circle Theater, 66
The Castle Inn, 119
Cenotaph for a Warrior, 9
Century of Progress exposition, Chicago (1933), 121
Chaplin Brothers Studio, 28
Charlie's Diner, 146
The Cheese House, 156–157
Chiat Day advertising agency, 88, 111
Chief Auto Supply, 165
Chili Bowl, 62, 64–65, 67
Chilitown Cafe, 62
Chimpanzee Farm, cover
Chrysler Building, 10
The Cider Barrel, 128, 130
Circle Tower Shopping Center, 11
CityWalk, 88, 173
Cliff Dwellers Cafe, 14, 54, 62, 63
Clifton's Cafeteria, 16, 94

The Club Car, 98–99
Club Car Restaurant, 15
Cobb's Chicken House, 15, 136–137
Coca-Cola Bottling Company, 11, 14, 15, 70, 98–99
The Coffee Cup, 89
The Coffee Pot, 112–113, 142
The Coliseum, 124
Colossal Elephant of Coney Island, 9, 115
Coney Island Hot Dog, 156–157
Cookie Jar, 85
Coon Chicken Inn, 148–149
The Cream Can, 63, 72–73
Cross Roads of the World, 14, 70, 99
Currie's Ice Cream, 76, 106–107

D

Dairyland, 139–140
The Darkroom, 15, 100
Delta Crest Nursery and Service Station, 93
The Derby Drive-In, 149
Derrah, Robert H., 14
Deschwanden's Shoe Repair, 108–109
Devils Gorge, 20–21
Dilly-Wagon Drive-In, 155
Dinah's, 68
Dino's Service Station, 158–159
Dinosaur Gardens, 173
Disney World, 172
The Do-Nut Hole, 15
The Dog, 134–135
Dog House, 107
Doggie Diner, 79, 108
The Donut Hole, 108–109
Dragons Gorge, 20–21, 23
The Dugout, 16, 90
Dunes Hotel, 171, 174

E

Edison Field, 172
Egyptian Theater, 6, 13, 14, 30, 35
Egyptian Village Cafe, 14
El Charro (The Sombrero), 149
El Miradero, 24–25
El Rancho Vegas, 171

El Sombrero Drive-In, 153
Elysian Park apartments, 55
Enchanted Island, 136–137
Excalibur Hotel, 171

F

Farmer John's Meat Packing Plant, 16
Fatty Arbuckle's Plantation Club, 14, 35, 45, 46
Feature Animation Building, 172
Fireplace, 45
The Fish Inn, 118, 132–133
Fleetwood Square, 84, 111
The Food Basket, 154
Freda Farms, 121
The Freezer, 13, 36, 62
Fry's Electronics, 170

G

The Garden of Allah, 96–97
Garden of Eden Date Shop, 89
Gay's Lion Farm, 14, 96–97
George A. Simpson Lunchboat, 128–129
The Giant Artichoke, 172
The Giant Barrel, 85, 89
Giant Cash Register, 118
Giant Orange, 67, 92–93
Girard Real Estate Development, 14, 47, 55
The Glacier, 7
Glengarry Castle, 25
The Golf Ball, 118
Goody Goody Coffee Pot, 138
Grace Baptist Church, 68, 93
Grand Canyon Electric Railroad, 20–21
Grand Central market, 8
Grauman's Chinese Theatre, 6, 13, 14, 48–49, 62
Green Dragon Colony, 24
Green Mill, 34, 45, 46

H

Haines Shoe House, 122
Halifax Creamery, 120–121
The Ham Tree, 34, 45

The Hamburger That Ate L.A., 87, 111
Hangman's Tree, 79
Hat 'n Boots Service Station, 122, 153
Hawaiian Gardens, 97
Hollywood Flower Pot, 5, 63, 79
The Hoosegow, 33, 45
Hoot Hoot I Scream, 15, 58–59, 63
The Hopper, 138
Hotel Tahquitz, 42

I

The Ice Castle, 46
Ice Cream Cannister, 112–113
The Ice Palace, 36, 46
The Iceberg, 142, 144–145
The Igloo, 15, 36, 46
The Igloo Lodge, 172
Ince Studios, 28, 35, 45
Indian head root beer stand, 128, 131
Indian Village, 42
Indian Village, KS, 112–113, 122–123
Irvin C. Willat Productions studio, 13, 26, 28, 45, 175

J

Jack Frost, Cinerama Dome, 170
Jail Cafe, 16, 78–79
Japanese palace (Bernheimers), 24, 25
Jerry's Cabin Cafe, 32–33, 45
Jesse James Cabin, 33, 45
The Jumbo Lemon, 67, 74–75

K

Kenyon's Desert Plunge, 52–53
Kid Blair's Showboat, 128
Kimo Theatre, 124
King's Tropical Inn, 14, 33, 45
The Kone Inn, 36
The Krotona complex, 22–23, 25

L

La Salsa, 164–165
Leaning Tower, Y.M.C.A., 158

Below: Left. **S.S. Grand View Point Hotel, Bedford, Pennsylvania ca 1932.** *Right.* **Pilot House, Copper Harbor, Michigan ca 1937.**

Leipzig Trade Fair booths, 114–115
Light of Asia, 115
Lighthouse Gardens, 45
Little America, 136–137
Little Mary's Realty, 29
The Lobster Trap, 139, 141
The Log Cabin Inn, 124
Longaberger Basket Company, 168–169, 170
Los Bãnos bathhouse, 24
Los Feliz Boulevard, 29
Lucy the Elephant, 114–115
Luxor pyramid hotel, 170–171, 174

M
Ma Perkins Chicken Inn, 158
Magnus Root Beer drive-in, 68
Mammy's Cupboard, 148–149
Mammy's Shack, 32–33, 45
The Mandarin Market, 14, 50, 62
Margo Leavin Gallery, 171
May Museum, 166
Mayan Theater, 6, 13, 14, 63
The Melon Patch, 135
MGM Grand Hotel, 171, 174
Miami Serpentarium, 156
The Midway Plaisance, 20–21
The Miner's Hat, 152–153
Mission Village, 32–33, 45, 63
Mizner, Herbert, 63
Monkey Farm, 33, 45
Montgomery's Country Inn, 29
The Motel Inn, 68, 92–93
Mother Goose Pantry, 13, 15, 16, 63, 68–69
The Mountains, 54
Moxie Bottle, 118
Muffler Men, 163–165
The Mushrooms, 16, 62–63

N
National Fishing Hall of Fame, 173
Nebraska State Capitol Building, 10
Nehi gas station, 116, 118
Nevada landing, 174
Noah's Ark, 86–87, 146–147

O
Ocean Park bathhouse, 23
Ocean Spray Cranberry, 138–139
The Oil Can, 72
The Old Log Cabin, 13, 24
The Orange Blossom, 74
Orange Box, 139–140
Orange Inn, 16
Orange World, 156–157

P
Pacific Savings, 14
Palazzo Zuccari, 9
Panama Pacific Exposition (1915), 23
Parker-Judge Decorating Company, 70–71
Persian Market, 45
Petaluma, The World's Egg Basket, 18–19
Petrified Wood Gas Station, 139, 141
Pharoah's Lost Kingdom, 170
Pickford, Mary, 66, 67
The Pickle Barrel, 128, 131
Pickle Bill's, 108
Pierre Voyageur, cover
The Pig Barbecue, 133
The Pig Cafe, 15, 16, 59
Polar Bear Frozen Custard, 146–147
Polks Dairy, 120–121
The Popcorn Ball, 118
The Pumpkin Inn, 56
Pumpkin Palace, 16, 56–57, 63
Punch and Judy, 64
The Pup Cafe, 7, 45, 63
Pyramid Cube University, 88–89

R
The Rabbit, 66
Ray L. Hommes Realty, 70–71

Recruit battleship, 116–117
Red Apple grocery store, 126–127
Richfield building, 10, 66
Rosicrucian Order, 26
Round House Cafe, 16, 62
Royal Barbecue Inn, 45

S
Samson's Tire Works, 7, 44–45, 62, 175
Sanders System drive-ins, 67, 76–77
Sanderson Stockings, 76, 103
Sans Souci, 24, 25
Santa Claus, CA, 105
Self Realization Fellowship, 26
Selig Studio, 28
Shell Oil Company, 137
Sherman Oaks Service Station, 85
The Ship Cafe, 20–21, 22–23
The Ship dance hall, 119
Ship restaurant in Venice, 20–21
The Shoe House, 156
The Showboat, 84, 110–111
Showboat Casino, 171, 174
Showboat Drive-In Theater, 128
The Shrine Auditorium, 22–23
Shutter Shack, 87, 110–111
Shutterbug, 15
Silver Castle, 12
Sisson's Coffee Pot, 142
Skyline Diner, 15
Soboba Hot Springs resort, 38–39, 52
The Sombrero (El Charro), 149
Sphinx gas station, 119
Sphinx head, 22
Sphinx Realty Building, 15, 60–61, 63
Stan's Lighting Distribution, 171
Stardust Hotel, 171
Steinhart Aquarium, 70

Streamline Diner, 70, 102–103
Streets of Paris, 137
Striper No. 1 Fish Stand, 132–133
The Stump Cafe, 118
Stump Cafe, 151
Sunset Towers, 10
Swedish Exposition (1907), 114–115

T
Tail o' the Pup, 15, 74, 76, 100–101, 176
Tam o' Shanter Inn, 14, 28, 29
The Tamale, 15, 63, 70
Taube Plumbing Supply, 86–87
Team Disney Building, 87–88, 111, 172
TeePee Barbecue Company, 54–55, 63
TeePee Drive-In, 42
Tehuantepec, 20
Television Store, 154
Theodore's School of Music, 105
The Theosophist's Commune, 22–23, 24
Thunderbird Hotel, 171
Tiree Castle, 42
The Toed Inn, 15, 16, 61, 63
Tomahawk TeePee, 158–159
Tom's Steak and Hogies, 164
Toonerville Trolley, 5, 87
Tower Auto Court, 42, 52
Tower Mart store, 173
Trancas Beach residence, 40
Tripoli Temple Shrine Mosque, 124
Trout Capitol of the World, cover
The Tuck Box, 68, 94
Tupper and Reed Building, 70, 94–95
Twin Barrels, 67, 84–85
The Twin Inns, 18
Twin Lakes Park, 52
Twist Inn, 116, 118
Twist o' the Mist, 168–169

U
"U Buy A Bond" submarine, 116–117

Umbrella Service Station, 16, 88
United Equipment Company, 84, 172
U.S. Royal Tires, 156
U.S. Tires, 44–45

V
Valley Gospel Center, 56–57
Van de Kamp's Bakery, 13, 26–27, 28, 62, 76
Venetian Garden, 15
Venice Scenic Railway, 23
Vico Gas Station, 128, 129

W
Wadhams Service Station, 118, 151
Walt's Restaurant, 139, 141
Wandover Will, 161
Warner, Jack, 63
Weismantel's Showboat, 128–129
Westwood Observation Tower, 50–51
White Castle, 12, 118
White Log Taverns, 13, 67, 90
White Tower, 12, 118
Wickenburg cowboy hat souvenir stand, 122
The Wigwam, 15, 30–31, 42, 102–103, 122–123
Wigwam Motel, 146, cover
William Penn Diner, 126
Wilshire Links, 67, 80–81
The Windmill, 124–125
Wolf's Lair, 30
Woodcutter's House and Workshop, 9
The World A Million Years Ago, 137
World's Fair, New York (1939), 121
Wynn's Airplane Tire Delivery, 166–167

Y
Ye Bull Pen Inn, 10, 67

Z
Zanzibar Cafe, 42
Zep Diner, 15, 63, 68
The Zulu Hut, 30–31, 42

Below: Left. **Marty's Showboat, Three Lakes, Wisconsin ca 1947.** *Right.* **S. S. Castle Rock, Smith River, California ca 1953.**

Gebhard's Notes

1. John R. Crossland, ed. *The Modern Marvels Encyclopedia* (London and Glasgow: Collins Clear-Type Press, 1938), p. 313.

2. "Palaces of The Hot Doges," *Architectural Forum*, vol. 63, August 1935, pp. 30–31.

3. *The Illustrated Directory of Oakland, California* (Oakland: The Illustrative Directory Co., 1896), pp. 25–26.

4. Abvert Forbes Sieveking, *Gardens Ancient and Modern* (London: Aldine House, 1899), p. 17. The shaping of trees and shrubs into geometric and other forms dates back to the early Egyptian period. See Richardson Wright, *The Story of Gardening* (New York: Dover Publications, 1963), p. 32.

5. In addition to the three French architects, Claude-Nicolas Ledous, Etienne Louis Boulée, and Jean Jacques Lequeu, who are the acknowledged masters of the late eighteenth-century Visionary architecture, there were the Germans David and Friedrich Gilly, Karl Friedrich von Schinke, the Britons Sir John Soane and Joseph Gandy, and the Americans Benjamin H. Latrobe and Thomas Jefferson. See Emil Kaufmann, "Three Revolutionary Architects, Boulée, Ledoux, and Lequeu," *Transactions of the American Philosophical Society*, vol. 42, part 3, (Philadelphia, 1952); *Visionary Architects: Boulée, Ledoux, Lequeu* (Houston: University of St. Thomas, 1968).

6. Theodore F. Laist, "Peculiar Architecture," *American Architect and Building News*, vol. 29, August 9, 1890, pp. 86–89; Clay Lancaster, *Architectural Follies in America* (Rutland, Vermont: Charles E. Tuttle Co., 1960), pp. 186–193; Julian Cavalier, "Elephants Remembered," *Historic Preservation*, vol. 29, January-March 1977, pp. 39–43. An elephant similar to that at Margate City was built by Lafferty at Coney Island.

7. Illustrated in *The Architect and Engineer*, vol. 26, October 1911, p. 105.

8. "Milk Bottle Architecture," *The Architect and Engineer*, vol. 35, January 1914, p. 113.

9. Kenneth M. Murchison, "As I See It," *The American Architect*, vol. 138, September 1930, p. 24.

10. *Ibid.*, 1930, p. 25.

11. Charles Harris Whitaker and Harley Burr Alexander, *The Architectural Sculpture of the State Capitol at Lincoln, Nebraska* (New York: Press of the American Institute of Architects, 1926).

12. David Gebhard, *The Richfield Building: 1928–1968*, (New York: The Atlantic Richfield Co., 1968), p. 16.

13. Robert H. Orr, "Sculptural Advertising," *The Architect and Engineer*, vol. 91, October 1927, p. 27.

14. Illustrated in *Signs of the Times*, vol. 68, June 1931, p. 31.

15. H. A. Wood, "Used Car Marketing," *Signs of the Times*, vol. 66, November 1930, p. 48; "Milwaukee, Wis.," *Signs of the Times*, vol. 77, August 1934, pp. 56–57.

16. H. H. Linsmith, "One Bulletin Display," *Signs of the Times*, vol. 72, September 1932, p. 13.

17. David Gebhard, "Life in the Dollhouse," *Bay Area Houses*, Sally Woodbridge (Editor) (New York: Oxford University Press, 1976), pp. 99–119.

18. "For Streamlined Structures," *Signs of the Times*, vol. 81, December 1935, pp. 12–14.

19. One of the richer sources of our knowledge of programmatic architecture is the *Official Gazette* of the U.S. Patent Office; especially the years from 1928 through 1935.

20. The White Tower Chain was established in Milwaukee in 1926. See Paul Hirshorn and Steven Izenour, *White Tower* (Cambridge, Mass.: M.I.T. Press, 1979).

21. The White Castle system was established in Wichita, Kansas, in 1921. It eventually spread east to New York City. See E. W. Ingram, Sr., *All This From a 5-Cent Hamburger* (New York: The Newcomer Society in North America, 1970). For examples of White Castle buildings see David Gebhard and Tom Martinson, *A Guide to Architecture in Minnesota* (Minneapolis: University of Minnesota Press, 1977). The Silver Castle system was established in Tulsa, Oklahoma, in 1936, and by 1941 units had been built throughout Oklahoma and parts of Texas.

22. See note 19.

23. J. Edward Tufft, "The Mother Goose Pantry," *Wayside Salesman*, vol. 1, November 1931, p. 20.

24. "White Log Taverns," *Pacific Coast Record*, June 1934, pp. 11 and 12; "Quick Lunch in California," *Fortune*, vol. 16, July 1937, pp. 90–94.

25. Sam F. Goddard, "From Footlights to Fireplaces," *Pacific Coast Record*, vol. 18, April 1927, pp. 21–22.

26. "New Studio in Novelty," *Los Angeles Express*, April 6, 1921, p. 19. This building was later remodeled and moved to Beverly Hills, and became known as the Spadena Residence.

27. *Ibid.*, 1921, p. 19.

28. The first of the Van De Kamp's Bakery buildings with the windmill motif was built in 1921 in Los Angeles at the corner of Western and Beverly Boulevards. The initial name of The Tam o' Shanter Inn was Montgomery's Country Inn.

29. "Tam o' Shanter," *Pacific Coast Record*, vol. 29, September 1938, pp. 14–15.

30. *Ibid.*, 1938, p. 14.

31. "Cross Roads of The World," *California Arts and Architecture*, vol. 51, January 1937, p. 24.

32. "Aztec Breathes of Olden Days," *Pacific Coast Record*, vol. 16, October 1925, pp. 1–2; Joe Minster, "Soboba Indian Village," *Pacific Coast Record*, vol. 18, July 1927, pp. 1–2.

33. Morrow Mayo, *Los Angeles* (New York: Alfred A. Knopf, 1933). The two pages of photos of programmatic buildings bear the caption "Some of The Bizarre Restaurants and Refreshment Stands which delight the eye and tickle the Palate of visitors to Los Angeles." See also "Weird Architecture Helps to Sell Ice Cream," *Popular Mechanics*, vol. 49, January 1928, p. 101; "Wayside Inns Around Los Angeles," *Wayside Salesman*, vol. 1, November 1930, pp. 20–21; "Many Unique Refreshment Stands Adorn Southern California Highways," *Wayside Salesman*, vol. 1, July 1930, pp. 16–17. "Palaces of The Hot Doges," *Architectural Forum*, vol. 63, August 1935, pp. 30–31.

34. Annette Del Zeppo and Jeffrey Stanton, *Venice, California, 1904–1930* (Venice, Calif.: ARS Publications, 1978).

35. "The Coca-Cola Plant, Los Angeles, California," *California Arts and Architecture*, vol. 50, November 1936, p. 43.

36. "All Aboard the Sky Liner," *Pacific Coast Record*, vol. 29, July 1938, p. 16.

37. "California Boom," *Life*, vol. 20, June 10, 1946, p. 31.

38. The form of the doughnut for a programmatic building dates from the 1939 New York World's Fair, where the respected firm of Skidmore and Owings designed with John Moss a Wonder Bakers building using this theme. See *Architect and Engineer*, vol. 137, January 1938, p. 8.

39. Illusionary signage which played off real buildings against perspective murals suggesting buildings and landscape was illustrated from time to time in the pages of *Signs of the Time*. For example, see the illustration of Vernor's Ginger Ale Building and sign in Flint, Michigan, *Signs of the Times*, vol. 74, August 1933, p. 24.

40. Robert H. Orr, "Sculptural Advertising," *The Architect and Engineer*, vol. 91, October 1927, p. 54.

41. Henry Russell Hitchcock, *The Architecture of H. H. Richardson and His Times* (New York: Museum of Modern Art, 1936), pp. 302–303.

42. "Tourism and Mobility," *Landscape*, vol. 9, no. 3, Spring 1962, pp. 1–27; "The Evolving Strip," *Landscape*, vol. 16, no. 3, Spring 1967, p. 2.

43. Robert Venturi, *Complexity and Contradiction in Architecture* (New York: Museum of Modern Art, 1965); and Robert Venturi, Denise Scott Brown, and Steven Izenour, *Learning from Las Vegas* (Cambridge, Mass.: M.I.T. Press, 1972). Another early exponent of programmatic architecture is the Viennese architect Hans Hollein, who in the early 1960s asked why we might not use the form of an aircraft carrier for a city, or the form of a spark plug or a Rolls Royce radiator grill for a high-rise building. See *Hollein*, catalogue published for the exhibition (Chicago: Richard Feigen Gallery, 1969). There have been several recent publications which have explored programmatic aspects of the commercial vernacular. These include Marc Treib, "Eye-Konism, Part 1," *Print*, Vol. 27, March/April 1973, pp. 68–73; "Eye-Konism, Part 2," *Print*, Vol. 27, May/June 1973, pp. 54–60, 104; John Baeder, *Diners* (New York: Abrams, 1978); Paul Hirshorn and Steven Izenour, *White Tower* (Cambridge, Mass.: M.I.T. Press, 1979); Daniel I. Vieyra, *Fill 'er Up: An Architectural History of America's Gas Stations* (New York: Collier Books, 1979); Richard J. S. Gutman and Elliott Kaufman, *American Diner* (New York: Harper and Row, 1979).

44. The Maurer Duck at Riverhead was illustrated and discussed in "Duck-Shaped Building Advertises Roadside Business," *Roadside Merchant*, vol. 5, May 1934, p. 7.

Photo Credits

Auburn University Archives: *116* • Automobile Club of Southern California: *41 top* • John Baeder Collection: *120 bottom, 123 top, 125 bottom, 128 bottom, 129 middle, 140 top, 143 top, 146 top, 147 top, 149 top left, 151, 152, 154 top, 155 top, 156 middle, 160, 176, 177* • Roger Beerworth: *169 bottom, 174 bottom right* • Bibliotheque National: *8 left* • Bison Archives/Marc Wanamaker: *19 top, 33 bottom right, 62, 63, 71 top, 89 bottom, 99, 104* • Marilyn Blaisdell: *22 top* • California State Library, Merge Collection: *77 bottom left, 81 top* • John and Gina Caparell: *168* • Corbis: *73, 132 bottom,* • Jeff Carr: *55, 22,* • Victoria Daly: *66, 85 top & middle* • FPG: *103 right, 133 top, 138 bottom, 140 bottom* • Abigail Gumbiner/Catchlight Photography: *175 bottom* • Richard Gutman: *139, 164 right top,* • Tillie Hattrup: *59 bottom* • Jim Heimann Collection: Frontispiece, *3, 4, 8 right, 9, 20, 21, 22 bottom, 23, 24, 24, 26top, 27, 28, 29, 30, 31 middle & bottom, 32, 33, 34, 35 top, 36 top left, 37, 39 bottom, 41 bottom, 44, 47 middle & bottom, 50 top, 52, 53, 54 bottom, 55 Top, 57, 58, 60, 61, 64, 67, 70, 72 bottom, 74, 75 top, 77 right, 78, 79, 81 bottom, 82, 86 top & bottom, 89 top, 90, 93, 94, 95, 96 top, 97, 98, 99 top, 100, 102 top, 103 top, 105, 106, 107, 108, 109, 110, 111, 114, 115, 118 bottom, 124, 131 top left & bottom, 136, 137, 140 middle, 141 bottom, 149 bottom, 153 bottom, 155 bottom, 156 top & bottom, 157, 161, 162, 163, 164, 165, 166, 170, 171, 172, 174 top left & bottom right, 176,177,180, endpapers* • Max Hurlbut: *174 bottom left* • Indiana Historical Society: *120 top, 142 top, 143 top* • Library of Congress: *75, 113, 121, 125 top, 134, 146 bottom* • Longaberger Company: *169 top* • Los Angeles Public Library, History Department: *2, 17, 42, 47 top left, 69 bottom, 80, 88* • John Margolies Collection: *120 middle, 126 bottom, 128 top* • National Archives: *69 top, 102 middle, 144, 153 top* • Tom Patchett, Track 16 Gallery, *148 top & middle* • Don Preziosi: *117, 118 top, 129 top & bottom, 130, 131 top right, 132 top, 139 top, 141 top, 142 bottom, 149 top right, 150, 154 bottom, 158, 159* • San Diego Historical Society: *12, 102 bottom* • Bruce Torrence: *31 top* • University of California, Santa Barbara: *38, 39 left and right* • University of Southern California Regional History Center: *43, middle left, 47 top right, 48, 54 bottom, 77 bottom, 113 bottom, 123 bottom, 126 top, 127 top, 138 top, 148 bottom* • University of Kentucky: *141 middle* • Delmar Watson Photography: *57 bottom, 58, 86 middle* • Westwood Historical Society: *51* • Whittington Collection: *7, 13, 16, 26 bottom, 35 bottom, 40, 43 top and middle left, 72 top, 96* • Arthur Whizin: *65* • Wichita Public Library, Local Histroy Section: *147 bottom* • The Williams Partnership: *6, 29 middle, 36 bottom right, 45* • Tom Zimmerman: *32 middle left, 33 top left, 36 top right, 50, top, 56, 59 top, 71 bottom, 176 second left*

Bibliography

BOOKS

Andrews, J. J. C., *The Well Built Elephant.* New York: Congdon & Weed, 1984.

Baeder, John. *Gas, Food, and Lodging.* New York: Abbeville Press, 1982.

Barth, Jack, Doug Kirby, Ken Smith, and Mike Wilkins. *Roadside America.* New York: Simon & Schuster 1986.

Blaisdell, Marilyn. *San Franciscania: Photographs of Three Worlds Fairs.* San Francisco: Marilyn Blaisdell Publishers, 1994.

Brownlow, Kevin, and John Kobal. *Hollywood the Pioneers.* New York: Alfred A. Knopf, 1979.

Cirigliano, Linda. *Hoot Mon! The Story of the Tam o' Shanter Inn.* Los Angeles: Lawry's Restaurants, Inc., 1995.

Cobb, Sally Wright, and Mark Willems. *The Brown Derby Restaurant.* New York: Rizzoli International Publications, 1996.

Dunlop, Beth. *Building a Dream: The Art of Disney Architecture.* New York: Harry N. Abrams, 1996.

Endres, Stacy, and Robert Cushman. *Hollywood at Your Feet: The Story of the World Famous Chinese Theatre.* Los Angeles: Pomegranate Press, 1992.

Ewald, Donna, and Peter Clute. *San Francisco Invites the World: The Panama Pacific International Exposition of 1915.* San Francisco: Chronicle Books, 1991.

Fisher, Joan E. *Automobile and Culture.* New York: Harry N. Abrams, 1984.

Hess, Alan. *Viva Las Vegas.* San Francisco: Chronicle Books, 1993.

Gebhard, David. *Robert Stacy-Judd.* Santa Barbara: Capra Press, 1993.

____. and Harriette Von Breton. *L.A. in the Thirties.* Salt Lake City: Peregrine Smith, 1975.

Jenks, Charles. *Bizarre Architecture.* New York: Rizzoli Books, 1979.

Kagan, Paul. *New World Utopias.* New York: Penguin Books, 1975.

Keller, Ulrich. *The Highway As Habitat: A Roy Stryker Documentation, 1943–1955.* Santa Barbara: University of California, Santa Barbara, 1986.

Liebs, Chester H. *Main Street to Miracle Mile: American Roadside Architecture.* Boston: Little, Brown and Company, 1985.

Longstreth, Richard. *City Center to Regional Mall: Architecture, the Automobile, and Retailing in Los Angeles, 1920–1950.* Cambridge, Massachusetts: MIT Press, 1997.

____. *The Drive-In, The Supermarket, and the Transformation of Commercial Space in Los Angeles, 1914–1941.* Cambridge, Massachusetts: MIT Press, 1999.

Margolies, John. *Fun Along the Road.* Boston: Bullfinch Press, Little Brown and Company, 1998.

____. *Home Away From Home.* Boston: Bullfinch Press, Little, Brown and Company, 1996.

____. *Pump and Circumstance.* Boston: Bullfinch Press, Little, Brown and Company. 1993.

____. *Signs of the Times.* New York: Abbeville Press, 1993.

Marling, Karal Ann. *The Colossus of Roads: Myth and Symbol along the American Highway.* Minneapolis: University of Minnesota Press, 1984.

Oberhand, Robert. *The Chili Bowls of Los Angeles.* Published for the Los Angeles Institute of Contemporary Art, Los Angeles, 1977.

Pennington, Lucinda and Wm. Baxter. *A Past To Remember. The History of Culver City.* Culver City,

1976.

Sears, Stephen. *The Automobile In America.* New York: The American Heritage Publishing Co., 1977.

Stanton, Jeffrey. *Venice California: Coney Island of the Pacific.* Venice, California: Donahue Publishing, 1993.

Venturi, Robert, Denise Scott Brown, and Steven Izenour. *Learning From Las Vegas.* Cambridge, Massachusetts: MIT Press, 1972.

Weitze, Karen J. *California's Mission Revival.* Los Angeles: Hennessey and Ingalls, 1984.

Williams, Dino, Alexa A. and Greg Williams. *The Story of Hollywoodland.* Los Angeles: Papavasilopoulos Press, 1992.

PERIODICALS

Allen, David. "No guiding light for those adrift in the desert." *The Sunday Press Dispatch/Victorville and Barstow,* California. March 2, 1997.

"Aztec Breathes of Olden Days." *Pacific Coast Record.* October 1925.

Bartolucci, Marissa. "Power." *Metropolis,* December 1994.

Betsky, Aaron. "Cartoon Character." *Los Angeles Times Magazine.* December 18, 1994.

Broersma, Dick. "Lasting Landmarks." *Daily Breeze.* April 19, 1995.

California Boom. *Life.* June 10, 1946.

"California Sunstruck Signs." *Hoilday.* January 1947.

Cardenas, Jose. "All Fixed Up." *Los Angeles Times.* May 25, 1996.

Carroll. Jerry. "Where Did The Giant Orange Go?" *San Francisco Chronicle.* July 29, 1973.

Chamberlain, J. H. "Denver Gets Something Different." *Signs of the Times.* May 1938.

"City May Not Have the Heart for This Building," *Los Angeles Times,* June 15, 1999, Section A– p.12.

Clinton, Paul. "Inside the Donut Hole." *San Gabriel Valley Weekly.* July 3, 1998.

"Colossal Elephant of Coney Island." *Scientific American,* July 11, 1885.

"Complaint Kicks In New Business," *Signs of the Time,* October 1949.

"Crossroads of the World." *California Arts and Architecture.* January 1937.

Dietz, Lawerence. "There Once Was A Woman Who Lived In A Shoe." *West Magazine of the Los Angeles Times.* November 30, 1969.

Doctoroff, Andrew S. "In Tarzana, Front-End Refinement." *Los Angeles Times.* January 22, 1987.

Ferguson, James. "White Log Taverns." *Pacific Coast Record.* June 1934.

"First Adaptation of Early Aztec Architecture to Modern Structural Designing." *Los Angeles Times.* May 5, 1912.

Godard, Sam F. "From Footlights to Fireplace." *Pacific Coast Record.* June 1927.

"Great American Roadside," *Fortune.* September 1934.

Gregory, Daniel P. "Billboard Buildings." *Sunset.* November 1992.

Graves, Amy Beth. "Tisket, tasket: Office in a Basket." *Tri-Valley Herald, Dublin, California.* March 2, 1998.

Gutis, Philip S. "Roadside Relics Of Early Auto Days Are Being Saved." *New York Times.* September 3, 1987.

____. "Suffolk to Preserve Its Landmark Duck." *New York Times.* August 26, 1987.

Harvey, Steve. "Eating Away at Oddball Architecture." *Los Angeles Times.* July 20, 1985.

____. "Only In L.A." *Los Angeles Times.* February 19, 1997.

Heimann, Jim. "Chili Climate." *Los Angeles Magazine.*

March 1997.

"How Glorified Ice Cream Stands Advertise and Sell the Product." *The Ice Cream Trade Journal,* March 1928.

Kelly, John F. "Santa Claus." *California Highways and Public Works.* March/April 1956.

Kuck, Lorraine. "Combines Sandwich Shack With Modern Road-House." *Pacific Coast Record.* February 1924.

Lacey, Marc. "Landmark Sign Is Threatened." *Los Angeles Times.* January 11, 1990.

Langdon, Phillip. "The Rebirth of the Bizarre." *Buffalo Evening News.* March 30, 1981.

Laug, Ruth. "That's Eatertainment." *Identity.* September/October 1995.

"Marathon Builds Octagonal Station at Tulsa." *National Petroleum News,* August 19, 1931.

Minster, Joe. "Soboba Indian Village." *Pacific Coast Record.* July 1927.

Moore, Kurt. "Ticky, Tacky." *Alaska Airlines Magazine.* April 1989.

"New Faces for Old Novelties." *Nation's Business.* November 1939.

"New Studio Is Novelty, Style Two Centuries Old Copied." *Los Angeles Express.* April 6, 1921.

"Only In Southern California: Claude Bell Builds Himself A Brontosaurus." *People Weekly.* June 23, 1975.

Paper, Henry. "A Hole In One." *California Living of the Los Angeles Herald.* February 24, 1985.

"Palaces of the Hot Doges." *Architectural Forum.* August 1935.

Pastier, John. "Chiat's New Look." *Adweek.* November 4, 1991.

"Plastic Statues Supplant Roadside Billboards." *Popular Mechanics.* October 1935.

Pope Meyer, Janice. "It Perks No More." *Indianapolis Courier-Journal Magazine.* April 24, 1960.

Reed, J. D. "Tacky Nostalgia? No, These Are Landmarks." *Time Magazine.* December 11, 1989.

"Roadside Shops That Tourists Can't Overlook." *American Weekly.* November 8, 1936.

Rockefeller, Mrs. John D., Jr. "Small Wayside Refreshmen-Stand Competition." *Ladies Home Journal.* November 1927.

Secter, Bob. "Upper Midwest takes stock in fiberglass fauna." *Los Angeles Times.* December 23, 1991.

Simon, Stephanie. "Metal Behemoths Punctuate Prairie Vistas In North Dakota." *Los Angeles Times.* August 24, 1999.

"Streamlined Diner." *Pacific Coast Record.* February 1941.

"Super Station Designed As Mosque," *National Petroleum News,* April 18, 1928.

Taylor, Frank. "Goodbye Harry Oliver." *Hollywood Studio Magazine,* September 1973. pp. 9–12.

"Teen Entrepreneur Turns Cool Profit With His Icy Cones." *Los Angeles Times.* October 11, 1983.

"Wandering Minstrel Rides Deluxe." *Los Angeles Times,* October 5, 1928.

"Weird Architecture Helps Sell Ice Cream." *Popular Mechanics.* January 1928.

Wiley, G. Harrison. "The House That Jack Builds." *The Motion Picture Director.* January 1926.

Wilson, Jane. "We Don't Know Where Ma Is, But We Got Pop On Ice." *West Magazine of the Los Angeles Times.* June 20, 1971.

"World's Queerest Eating Places." *Science and Invention.* April 1931.

Additional resources for material are various issues of the *Wayside Salesman, Pacific Coast Record,* the newsletter of the Society for Commercial Archaeology, and the Roadside America Web site.

For those who are interested in the California Crazy concept and aficionados of the American commercial roadside, the Society of Commercial Archaeology is a terrific organization which locates and supports all aspects of the built American commercial environment. Membership information can be obtained from their Web site at www.sca-roadside.org.

Acknowledgments

Producing books is a complex, time consuming, and collaborative effort and the following are among the innumerable people who have made *California Crazy and Beyond* possible. Special thanks go out to: Alan Rapp, my editor at Chronicle, for once again shepherding me through another book project with ease and expertise. As well as the rest of the Chronicle staff including designer Vivien Sung. Cindy Vance for her enthusiasm and one of the smoothest production jobs ever. Blue, Liz, and Adrian of Artworks who did it again, producing the innumerable transparencies for this project. Tina Gloub for working on the proposal comps. Glenn Parsons for his cover comps. Mrs. David Gebhard for generously allowing the reprint of her husband's essay. John Baeder, Richard Gutman, John Margolies, Marc Wanamaker, Delmar Watson, and Tom Zimmerman for the generous use of their amazing archives and for being just nice guys. Dace Taub of USC's Regional History Center, and Carolyn Cole of the Los Angeles Public Library for their expertise, superior collections, and curatorial acumen. Roger Beerworth for shooting and supplying me with his vacation "snapshots." Victoria Daly and Steve Turner for their photo album which included two obscure programmatic discoveries. The Williams family, Dino, Greg, and Alexa, for the unselfish access to their collection. Matt Roth of the Automobile Club of Southern California for his friendship, support, and always keeping an eye out for images. Jeff Carr and Don Preziosi for their encyclopedic collections of postcards and images and their generous usage. Chris DeNoon, whose research twenty years ago is still invaluable. Max Hurlbut, wherever you are. Patricia Buckley who some twenty years ago sent me a series of snapshots of her Midwest "finds." An additional heartfelt thanks goes out to all of those folks who have contributed to this edition of *California Crazy* with their images, advice, research, and continuing efforts in supporting, documenting, and preserving our roadside culture including Steve Anaya, Gary Baseman, Brad Benedict, Ralph Bowman, Andraeus Brown, Brian Butko, Gina and John Caparell, Dan DePalma, Michael Doret, Lenny Davidson, John English, Steve Harvey of the *Los Angeles Times*, Alan Hess, Neil and Melinda Joeck, Jeff Labovitz, the Los Angeles Conservancy, Chris Nichols, Todd Schorr, Laura Smith, Kathy Staico, The Society of Commercial Archaeology, and Carolyn Mannon Huber and Kirsten Combs of the Westwood Historical Society. And finally to all those who continue to share their information, enthusiasm, and passion for these buildings, signs, and the commercial environment which make it possible for this phenomenon to be kept alive.

Call it divine intervention, positive karma, or dumb luck, the author has an epiphany as the Wienermobile passes Randy's Donut, La Cienega and Manchester boulevards, Inglewood, March 1994.

As always, to Roleen and Zoë.